RETO   ANDREA   SAVOLD
Solothurn, Switzerland in 1949. He is a director and actor, best known for his films *Stella da Falla* (1971) and *Lydia* (1968). In his early years he was celebrated as a top talent of auteur film, having been commissioned by Swiss television to make a film aged 22 (*Stella da Falla*) of which he had written the screenplay. *Stella da Falla* was the official Swiss entry to the Locarno Film Festival. He trained in Eurythmy under Elena Zuccoli at the Goetheanum, Swizerland. From 1981, he developed Gideon Spicker Verlag, where he was responsible for the publishing of Herbert Witzenmann's writings. Today he heads Das Seminar – Sozialästhetische Schulungsstätte, Basel, founded by Witzenmann in 1973. Having co-founded the Solothurn Steiner School, he later taught seven different subjects within the Basel State School. He is the father of three daughters.

The Future Art of Cinema

Rudolf Steiner's Vision

Reto Andrea Savoldelli

TEMPLE LODGE

Translated from German by Matthew Barton

Temple Lodge Publishing Ltd.
Hillside House, The Square
Forest Row, RH18 5ES

www.templelodge.com

Published in English by Temple Lodge in 2020

Originally published in German under the title *Rudolf Steiner über das Kino – zur Genealogie des Films* by SeminarVerlag, Basel, in 2017

A CIP catalogue record for this book is available from the British Library

ISBN 978 1 912230 40 2

Cover by Morgan Creative
Typeset by Vman Infotech Pvt Ltd., Chennai, India
Printed and bound by 4Edge Ltd., Essex

To advance the spirit in cinema…

Dedicated to the future filmmakers who read this study

'Similarly, he went to the cinema from time to time to see especially typical and characteristic new films. And he pondered on how one might use the medium of film in a culturally progressive way. But at the same time he saw more clearly than anyone the dangers attendant on blind enthusiasm for the cinema.'

– Herbert Hahn, *Rudolf Steiner: Wie ich ihn sah und erlebte*

Contents

Prologue

Joseph Vogelsang leaves the hermitage near Solothurn and sets out for home. He passes the cave where Saint Verena lived many centuries ago, passes the hermit's dwelling and the recreated Garden of Gethsemane, the scene where the disciples succumbed to sleep on that dark night, passes the rock tomb of Mary Magdalene and the three crucifixes of Solothurn's Golgotha, crossing himself as he does so. Nearby is the Church of the Cross, a smaller-scale recreation of the Church of the Holy Sepulchre in Jerusalem. The whole gorge is a single, walkable shrine, and for Vogelsang the precious artwork to which he wishes to devote his genius. *A sacred landscape which all human beings should see, wherever they may live!*

He heads for his workshop close by, and starts to make a scaled-down model of the recreated landscape. He wants to copy the whole hermitage, along with the hermit's cell and the stream full of trout dividing the gorge's two chapels. He integrates all this into a peep-box.[1] Once this is finished, he will push it before him on fixed struts, like a wheelbarrow, through Europe's market squares.

Many followed Vogelsang's prompting to look into the peep-box through one of its two openings: either through window glass on the left or through the magnifier on the right. Those who desired a more intense experience of space and time travel, got Vogelsang to open a little doorway in the side of the box: through this they could light a candle in Verena's chapel and pull on a string to make the little bell ring out over the cliffs.

Accounts of Vogelsang's wanderings trace his journey as far as Königsberg (today's Kaliningrad in Russia). The guest book which he always placed next to the peep-box on the table he was sitting on to wait for curious visitors, has been preserved. It even contains words of praise from the nobility of the day: from Kaiser Ferdinand in Prague to Baden's grand duchy, and from Hessen, from the Queen of Hannover, to the Queen of the Netherlands, whom Vogelsang visited in Interlaken with his peep-box. Two entries in the guest book are dated in the year of Rudolf Steiner's birth:

- Their Majesties, the widowed Queen of Prussia and Her Royal Highness the Grand Duchess Mother of Meklenburg, and the Princesses, daughters of the Beloved Wife of Prince Karl of Prussia, today viewed Herr Vogelsang's interesting represen-tations, whereupon all accord him due honour for having copied nature with such skill. Potsdam, 23 May 1861
- The microsculptural depictions of Herr Vogelsang met with my liveliest interest. Accomplished in most artistic fashion, with near-incomprehensible subtlety of depicted details, the whole, through the profoundly Goethean sensibility of its creator — whose whole soul lives and weaves in the nature he thus portrayed — is elevated into a true work of art. The incomparable recreation, both in the character of the whole and in the accuracy of the subtlest details, makes these studies of the very greatest interest also for the natural-scientific enquirer.
- Jena, 13 December 1861, signed Professor M.R. Schleidenbach, professor in Jena

Around a century later, the little boy I was at the time also peered into Vogelsang's peep-box. At this period it was relegated to a dark, more or less unnoticed corner under the large stairway of the Solothurn Museum of Art. And once again, someone lost themselves in gazing at Vogelsang's miraculous, miniature world. And since I, unlike most of Vogelsang's former customers, was deeply familiar with the Verena Gorge as a nearby destination for trips undertaken by the pious Seraphic Franciscan Sisters, who brought me up in my early years, it spoke very tellingly to my awakening imagination as an infant school pupil. My soul immersed itself in Vogelsang's box, and hovered amongst the familiar landmarks that it saw there in strangely altered form.

Many years later, the enthusiasm I shared with Vogelsang for the Solothurn Hermitage reappeared in a scene of my film, *Stella da Falla* (1971).[2] There, the film's chief protagonist, who ultimately calls herself *Stella da Falla*, walks side by side with Brother Niklaus — the actual hermit officiating at that time — through the Verena Gorge. In one scene he recites the following sentences from a gorgeously illustrated Bible:

> And the disciples came to him and asked, Why dost thou speak in parables to them? But he answered them, saying, Because it is given you to comprehend the secrets of the heavenly kingdom, but to them this is not given; for he who has, to him will be given unstintingly; but he who does not have, from him will be taken even the little he possesses. Therefore do I speak in parables to them, because they see and do not see, hear and do not hear or understand.

'See, and yet not see or understand.' We will go on to discover how this relates to cinema.

1

In the year 1900 there was no cinema yet in Berlin. But by 1920, four hundred designated 'cinema theatres' could be found in the city. That year, three and a half million people went to German cinemas every day. Vogelsang's peep-box had long since become obsolete. The active imagination I required as a young boy to awaken Vogelsang's 'snow globe' landscape to life was served on a plate to cinema-goers.

As early as 1837, Daguerre and Niépce had developed photographic reproduction. After the zoetropes, in which, for instance, a galloping horse was painted in 12 different phases of movement, and appeared to the viewer peering through a slot at the revolving drum as the horse in actual motion, Ottomar Anschütz used photographs as single images of movement sequences. In 1879 he invented the mechanism of the instant shutter integral to the film camera. His 'electro-tachyscope' considerably enhanced the naturalism of the visual spectacle he had presented at funfairs. Towards the end of the century, Europe and America were in feverish competition, with all minds, seemingly, focused on offering humanity the cinematic experience.

After celluloid roll film replaced photographic sheet film around 1890, roughly a dozen people, with the teams around them, were competing to produce the first commercially viable film show. Among them were unfunded loners such as Louis le Prince from Metz in France (a friend of Daguerre) who in October 1888, in a suburb of Leeds, was able to produce the first film ever with his recently patented camera. Called *Roundhay Garden Scene*, only a few seconds of it have survived.[3] Two years later, by now awarded American nationality, Le Prince disappeared without trace shortly before moving to New York, on his last train journey to Paris. No one has ever found out what happened to him. Two years later, in America, his son Alphonse, who also figured in *Roundhay Garden Scene*, lost his life during a duck shoot. At the time, as his father's representative, he was entangled in a court case of many years' standing for lucrative patent rights against the powerful inventor and entrepreneur, Thomas Alva Edison. All possible means were used to contest the success of these early film productions. Frantic competition in technical inventions was at full throttle, with a view to the expected commercial success.

From 1 November 1895, the Skladanowsky brothers showed their first eight short films to around 1500 people at the Varieté Winter Garden in the centre of Berlin, as the culmination of a daily programme of acrobats, fire-eaters, fortune tellers and conjurors. The films, lasting 15 minutes, included the famous *Boxing Kangaroo*. But until the beginnings of digital film technology from the 80s onwards, technical problems remained for all entrepreneurial competitors, and concerned ways to avoid flickering, to keep film presentation smooth, to maintain picture clarity, and to achieve the minimum frequency physiologically necessary for the human eye of roughly eighteen images per second. Only then could viewers experience movement simulation rather than the stroboscopic flare of individual images. The funnier the slapstick, the more effective was the illusion of 'true-to-life' movement.

On 5 November 1895, the editor of Berlin's *Staatsbürger* newspaper reported as follows on an evening at the Winter Garden:

> The finale of the performance shifts to the smaller stage of the bioscope. The ingenious technician here uses edifying still photographs and presents them in magnified form, but in living not frozen movement. The devil knows how he does this.

Two months later, the Skladanowskys were present at the first film show by the Lumière brothers, on 31 December 1895, in the Grand Café in Paris, and were compelled to observe that their technology was inferior to that of the Lumière brothers. It was very hard for anyone to appreciate the advantage of their own technology initially or even later on, since it appeared too complex. I'm thinking of the possibility, by using two intermittent film projectors, of avoiding

Cameramen in front of Berlin's City Palace, 1907

the otherwise inevitable incursion of the black space between frames (which gave rise to the flicker effect). A film viewer remains unaware that he is staring into the dark for around a third of the film's running time because his retina does not register the optical dissolves. (I will assume that the reader is familiar with the Maltese Cross technique used by the Lumières.) In the Duplex process employed by Skladanowsky, by contrast, the projection screen was continually illumined without the intervening fade-to-blacks.[4]

2

And where does Rudolf Steiner come into all this? In 1895 he lived not far from the Varieté Winter Garden and, from Berlin, in subsequent years, he observed the triumphant progress of cinema.

Before I begin to reproduce his comments on cinema — few and sparing compared to his entire published *oeuvre*, which encompasses over 350 volumes — I want to say this: My own film practice and reflections on cinema, and the visual media that later emerged from it, started when I was 16. I only became acquainted with Rudolf Steiner's thoughts much later on. What I have to say about them thus relates not only to Steiner's evaluation of the media phenomenon, of which anthroposophists are largely unaware, but at the same time highlights an accord with my own insights and intentions as these were documented already in the early seventies. My accounts of the epistemology and philosophy of media were published in a wide range of different journals and have not yet been compiled in one place.[5] (See Appendix 1 on the epistemology and philosophy of film.)

3

As we embark on an exploration of the nature of cinema, it is also important to briefly examine the premises of an ideological psychology whose reality-distorting assumptions and materialistic analyses are generally accepted by both producers and directors and figure at the hub of western cinema.

As early as 1874, Franz Brentano, an important precursor of psychological research founded on inner observation, pointed to the inadequacy of research methods such as that of behavioural psychology, which had begun to develop in English-speaking countries at the time.[6] This school sought to replace the direct, empirical study of inner processes with the statistical analyses conducted on test subjects that scientifically oriented psychologists had at their disposal. Instead of applying a scientifically developed, observational discipline, the forming of conceptual hypotheses and their verification, to the perceptual sphere of introspection, their unfounded fear that this would lead to something 'unscientific' led to statistically exploitable compilations of stereotypical answers to standardized questions. Using these, they sought to find a basis for effectively influencing behaviour through stimulus and inducement, so as to bring about the greatest possible common good by means of 'reasonable compulsion'. Despite the palpable scientific inadequacy of this approach, behaviourist psychology was a great 'success' in the recruitment and conditioning of management staff in large companies, in the military, politics and secret services, as well as in commercial advertising. Its methodological impact is still to be found everywhere today in questionnaires such as those employed for market research purposes, whose findings reveal the same relativizing lack of definition and an invariable need for further interpretation.

The questions are intentionally kept porous since the responder is not intended to think so much as to reveal his subconscious desires, opinions and impulses.

B.F. Skinner, one of the originators of the behaviourist approach — which though crazy still possesses methodology — formulates the following demand in *Beyond Freedom and Dignity*, an astonishingly highly-regarded book:

> Only by dispossessing [man of autonomy] can we turn to the real causes of human behaviour. Only then can we turn from the inferred to the observed, from the miraculous to the natural, from the inaccessible to the manipulable.

Skinner tries to repudiate ideas he has no liking for — about a freedom of cognition that he denies — and resolve them into forms of behaviour that operate according to instinctive stimulus and response mechanisms, having previously studied these in the behaviour of rats and pigeons, his preferred 'guinea pigs'.

In the work of Harvard Utopian Skinner, power and manipulation replace truth and self-knowledge as paradigms governing the transfer of scientific research techniques to psychological research in a way quite foreign to science. Like the old metaphor of the ostrich, truth and self-knowledge cannot be discovered in this outlook: what we do not acknowledge or seek cannot be found to exist. As mentioned earlier, the behaviourist image of man influenced many successful directors in the old Hollywood. In their view of cinema the object is to 'entertain' people by creating suggestive and alluring cinematic sequences, in contrast with the hopes of a minority that the cinema would give expression to a new artform. These latter felt themselves poorly 'entertained' by the mass product which, they felt, marginalized them as inconsequential bystanders. By exploiting anti-organic interventions in the physiology of the human senses (we will speak of this further in a moment), efforts were made to continually perfect a mass-market and therefore profit-oriented form of 'entertainment'.

John Huston, one of the most successful directors of classical Hollywood, once put it like this:

> To me the ideal film — which I've never succeeded in making —
> would be as though the reel were behind one's eyes and you
> were projecting it yourself, seeing what you wish to see. This
> has a great deal in common with thought processes... That's why
> I think the camera is an eye as well as a mind. Everything we do
> with the camera has physiological and mental significance.[7]

Further comments of a similar nature can be found in quotations
from William Friedkin: 'There are only three reasons people go
to the movies: to laugh, to cry, or to be scared. The latter is my
preference.' Or Alfred Hitchcock: 'The Chase seems to me to be the
ultimate expression of the film medium.' Then also Béla Balázs:
'Eroticism is the cinematic theme par excellence, its most intrinsic
subject.'[8] Thus each of these has pursued their own particular
obsession with the aim of realizing it cinematically in ever better
ways.

By contrast, my own statement to the Swiss Film Commission
(to promote the film project *You don't step twice in the same river*
or *After me will come the one who was before me*) sounded almost
naively optimistic:

> Countering this materialistic cultural stance, which has taken
> almost exclusive hold on the cinematic means of production, a
> current will now gradually emerge within the history of cinema
> that focuses on ensouling film as opposed to rendering it demonic
> (through coldly calculating, impersonal and power-seeking
> technology). The film camera and the microphone will come into
> the hands of people who are moved by heartfelt moral impulses,
> and who love film for its as yet scarcely tapped capacities to
> depict inner realities. Technical aids will lose their coldness,
> camera and microphone will become extensions of our sense
> organs, screen images will render visible the living soul in its
> primary activities, and image sequences, montage, will reveal a
> pattern woven from spiritual imaginations, that bear the stamp
> of an artist (not of a computer), whose organic logic will resemble
> that of a rose or a lion...

This programmatic statement from April 1973, which I can no
longer uphold in the form it took then, was driven by the desire to

establish an ideal at odds with that of Huston's view of cinematic entertainment, which seeks to suppress any self-examination on the part of the viewer. I was criticizing Huston, and with him all mass-market film directors, for the means they used in trying to develop a kind of substitute drug for states of self-oblivion, but in general I shared the view that a good film helps lift viewers out of their habitual, daily thoughts. To enliven themselves inwardly, I thought, they should be allowed to lose themselves in the cinema.

I had not yet more carefully scrutinized this desired state of 'self-oblivion'. Such examination becomes necessary if we are to distinguish the process of gradually liberating ourselves from the body through spiritual activity from that of a media-induced 'detachment from reality'.

4

Let us now turn to a few comments originating in the early era of cinema, by people whose emotional involvement in this newly emerging phenomenon can seem astonishing to us today. Yet it should be remembered that this was the very first time, after many millennia of artistic depiction — from the caves of Lascaux and Altamira to Monet and Picasso — that moving images 'resembling reality so closely as to be confused with it' had arisen in the field of narrative art. 'The suggestion of the film is founded on erasing the illusory character of its representation' said the Hungarian Marxist, Béla Balázs in his early theory of film entitled *Visible Man or The Culture of Film* (1924).

At the first screening of an 8mm film entitled JIPA ('Boy in Puberty') which I had made with a few school friends at the age of 16, I wrote on the wall of the improvised cinema the following sentence from Balázs's work: 'Film is the redemption of outer reality from the chaos of the random and transient.' A school friend's friend, who was ten years older than me, came up to me after the preview and asked me urgently: 'But what do you mean by "outer reality"?' My confusion, and inability to answer his question properly, intensified over the next few days into a troublesome irritant. And yet I saw ever more clearly how much I myself was implicated in what I had conceived to be this 'outer reality'.

I mention this personal experience to show to what degree the thoughts attendant on the birth of cinema seem to me to contain the primary task of learning to distinguish between inner and outer, between I and world, and also between essence and appearance. My attempt back then to understand the technical environment of cinema led to my first profound experience of my barriers to knowledge, which at that time seemed to me to be insuperable.

The first phase of 'film philosophy', in which these fundamental questions were pursued, albeit in a usually very superficial way, concluded in 1960 with the important work by the American Siegfried Kracauer, entitled *The Theory of Film*. Kracauer, too, subtitled his book with Balázs's formulation, 'The Redemption of Physical Reality'. In the period after this, academic discourse on film was dominated for several decades by French media theory, influenced by linguistics, semiology and psychoanalysis.[9] None of these — mostly Marxist — intellectuals could conceal the fact that their love of film, cultivated for the purposes of sociological and semantic discourse, also gave them welcome cause to eagerly visit the cinema. Various efforts to decipher the vocabulary of film language so as to assign cinema its high status in the orders of the arts (in France, after all, 'le cinéma' had been elevated to a 'seventh art') seeped away like water through the fingers of their speculative abstractions.

The theory of Marxist materialism accords concepts no reality except by reference to sensory experience. In the shadowy form in which this theory acknowledges the ordinary mind, it makes no headway either. Given that sensory experience appears to give theorizing intellectualism an, as it were, materialistic-cum-mystical assurance of reality, film images can seem more fully imbued with reality than the concepts and ideas whose shaping forces create reality by connecting with active, observing thinking. A few decades already before their Nazi successors, the leaders of Marxist-Leninist hegemony turned enthusiastically to the newly emerged 'proletarian' means of communication as a welcome tool of their propaganda. In the context of materialistic interpretations of culture, in the Soviet Union the state supported film on a large scale, and this gave rise to renowned early works of Russian cinema (Eisenstein, Pudovkin et al.). As early as 1919, the world's first film school was founded in Moscow, the Gerasimov Institute of Cinematography. Lenin saw in cinema an artistic herald of the classless society, and Balázs, in his first, widely disseminated work on film theory, linked film theory and political propaganda together in unmistakable fashion: 'Film will only be able to fulfil the potential it harbours and develop into a really great artform if the general development of our social milieu creates a cultural atmosphere that has an affinity with it.'

Rudolf Steiner, as a scientific Goetheanist, initially sought in the cinema experience the primary or archetypal phenomenon underlying it:[10]

> I have studied this; especially during the war years where film campaigns were waged on behalf of all sorts of things, one could see how eagerly people drank in film productions. I was not concerned with observing the films themselves so much as their audiences. And it became very apparent how film simply lies centrally within the whole programme of humanity's materialization, in as much as materialism is in a sense infused into people's habits of perception.[11]

If we now consider the quest to gain adequate understanding of the medium of film in the early years of its emergence, in the form of various comments made at the time,[12] we discover the vehemence with which cinema was rejected and demonized on the one hand, and loved and glorified on the other. This emotionality is often indicative of the underlying vicious circle set in motion by employing unsuitable means of cognition. It allows no distanced view of the medium but draws arguments from unexamined impulses of feeling. Thus Konrad Lange ought to have known that European theatre had staged all kinds of misdeeds and atrocities from an arsenal of possible crimes; nevertheless he waxes indignant about cinema for the following reason: 'If anything can be called gross mischief then it must certainly be the public representation of actions prohibited by criminal law.' Without examining this premise more closely, he assumes that the crimes portrayed in film are 'more real' than stage murders, and uses this to justify his indignation about such 'gross mischief'.

Painters and writers, as artists who particularly cultivate an ensoulment of sense impressions, have often expressed their antipathy to the medium. Today, such objections can scarcely be made any longer, and would no doubt elicit a general shaking of heads at such an outmoded outlook and its vain efforts to turn the clock back. 'It is a magnificent toy, it is true,' said Franz Kafka, 'but I cannot endure it. Perhaps I am too visually oriented. The cinema hinders vision. Films are iron blinds.'

The painter Edvard Munch had something else in mind when he said, 'Film will be inferior to painting until people can set up their cameras in heaven or hell.' Naturally he wasn't speaking of some filmic set of heaven or hell, already in plentiful supply at the time, but of the of the raw material of film as a sensory vehicle for expressing dramatic inner human states, which Munch conveyed more 'through' than in his paintings. The reason for this lies in the way mechanization of perception helps suppress the sensory-moral aspect (Goethe) of a visual impression, something we will examine more closely.

While visiting an exhibition devoted to the paintings of Monet at Beyeler Foundation (Basel),[13] I was struck by a vivid experience. As I looked at the originals I became aware that I had never *seen* them before, despite having seen numerous colour prints of his work in the past. The originals I had before me differed to a striking and confusing degree from the reproductions as I recalled them. In the photographic copy, what had passed from the painter's awareness into the colour and form qualities of the original, was nowhere to be found. Yet the latter, precisely, struck me as being the true soul of each painting.

I spent a long time in front of a series of different 'river moods' of the Seine at Giverny, which Monet's brush had conjured on the canvas in the finest colour transitions. The white-blueish greys of works painted in the early morning mist displayed weak contrasts only and, in the secondary creative activity of the viewer thus directly invoked, revealed the painter's inward artistic apprehension. (I freely admit that these impressions made me weep.) Here a miracle of aesthetically enhanced emancipation from sensory torpor held sway, allowing the spirit of the cool river, the play of light and water at the banks of the Seine, in which Monet's mind had long ago been absorbed, to be reborn in the observer.

After this I went to the basement to see a video installation by Thomas Brunner specially created for the exhibition. On a screen measuring 18 metres in breadth, subdivided into three or four segments, Brunner had kaleidoscopically projected interchanging sections from early French black-and-white films, in order to document the reciprocal influence of Impressionist painters and the new film medium in a collage cut to a soundtrack of Arvo Pärt's *Fratres*. I watched the whole 30 minutes of the show before going upstairs again to see Monet's images once more. Yet they had completely vanished! I no longer recognized them! It was as if they had in the meantime been replaced by colour prints instead. Penned in by the great crowd of viewers, I would have needed a long time to allow my previous, soulfully breathing mode of looking to unfold again. Struck and disturbed by this insight, I left the exhibition hurriedly.

Rudolf Steiner:

> Through the scientific mode of thinking we become accustomed to conceiving of natural laws, and through these natural laws we explain the natural phenomena we perceive with our senses. And now we look at the human organism, and also view it as if it could be comprehended by applying natural laws to it. But this is exactly like regarding a picture created by a painter in terms of the substance of its colours, by the strength of adherence of the colours to the canvas, by the way in which these colours can be applied to the canvas and so on. Yet none of these things get to the heart of what the painting reveals. What the painting manifests embodies laws completely different from those that can be gained from the above-mentioned perspectives...[14]

Steiner notes that the film viewer (and this applies to a still greater degree to the consumer of the digital entertainment industry) is excluded from the 'lawfulness of pictorial manifestation', and is instead compelled to dwell in the lower stratum of thinking in fixed effigies, reflections, which, as film has technically evolved, are 'post-produced' to an ever greater degree.

Like the difference between image and reflection, there is a similar difference between musical sound and its electronic repro-duction. Based on long musical experience, the major conductor,

Sergiu Celibidache has convincingly described this fact.[15] It took courage to realize this insight in practice since Celibidache's refusal to have the concerts he conducts recorded and marketed was associated with considerable financial losses. Celibidache has nothing in general against producing, recording and listening to technically created music, but he objected to the dulling of awareness of the distinction, apparent to inner observation, between that and technically unsupported music directly created in the presence of an active listener. The denial of such a distinction was for him itself the result of a severe impairment of musical experience.

Many years ago — on 14 September 1972, to be precise — during a film discussion following screening of my film, *Stella da Falla* at the student film club at Windisch Technical College (Switzerland), I made a remark that was often quoted afterwards:

> I strive for film in which consciousness of the sequencing is united, as by mathematical proof, with the absolute and intrinsic nature of liberated vision's inner creation of images. In other words, I try to find the rational, 'counter-nature' unity of a dream created by thinking, the ever more complete expression of names.

What follows aims to answer the question as to whether the ideal thus formulated is meaningful and whether it can be realized. Denial of the manipulative nature of film technology would render an answer impossible. Benno Ruttenauer no doubt sensed something of this when he wrote: 'The cinematograph, like everything substantially mechanical, embodies a more anti-cultural than culture-enhancing tendency. Compared to this, the roughest circus remains an art institute.'

Fascination with the cinema is not solely due to its capacity to be a *bioscope*, that is to reproduce 'living movement', and thus to achieve a high degree of pictorial naturalism, but also its ability to meet the opposite need — for unreality, for an experience of 'impossible', fantastical worlds and for enriching or reinvigorating impoverished and narrowed habits of perception. In Paris, Lumière set his film camera up on some boulevard or other, focused it on a tree, pressed the trip, and, when the film was projected later, took childlike pleasure in having so clearly captured the play of sun-light on fine leaves moving in the wind. His contemporary Méliès, on the other hand, created films with nothing but his imagination, and took pleasure in the technical apparatus that allowed him to render his dream-worlds visible. Thus with a sandbox, puppets and the first film tricks, he created his *Journey to the Moon*, the prototype of all space-fiction films. In fact, the silence of the silent movie increased the sense he sought of reverie and removal from daily life.

> In the first years of its emergence, film nourished the yearnings of people to experience daily reality differently. In its images they sought not an intensified physical reality but a distance from it. A huge pile of plates was impossibly balanced until, at the most unexpected moment, they collapsed and broke silently into pieces. Back then people would still double up with laughter at the fact that they could see what was happening but not a sound could be heard from it. (Rudolf Harms in *Philosophie des Films*, 1926)

The French philosopher Gabriel Marcel even assigns film the power

> to deepen our connections with this earth, our dwelling place, and to shape them more inwardly. And I would even say that, as someone who tends to tire of things I habitually see, or in other words, no longer actually see at all, this power intrinsic to cinema literally seems redemptive (quoted in Kracauer, p. 394).

For Siegfried Kracauer, this idea of Marcel's contains the culture-renewing meaning of cinema: 'The remedy to counter the sort of abstraction that has become widespread under the influence of science is experience — experience of things in their tangible reality.'

In these remarks too, the lack of a sustainable view of the world and reality is palpable, so that it is hard to know what to make of the thought of a 'cinema experience…of things in their tangible reality'. And when Gabriel Marcel suggests that the developing abstraction of the sense world is to be seen in his personal tendency to view things 'habitually', the least dose of an hallucinogenic drug could have made his error clear to him. The slightest disturbance to the brain's chemical balance turns a finger into a lindworm, the chirrup of cicadas into angelic song, and the sofa into a monster that engulfs its occupant. And all this without any 'deepening of our connection to the earth'.

And when Kracauer adds that science inevitably, as by an inner law, leads to a thinning of experiential reality, this too is a very one-sided statement. A science that does not stop halfway will inexorably and hugely expand the field of experience. In fact, the kind of science that penetrates the reality of spirit will be able to comprehend the *abstract* character of a *spirit-devoid experience of things*, which was Kracauer's view of science. Long before Marcel, a different philosopher described this fact. I am thinking of Hegel, who replied to a student's objection that he could not form a picture of the philosopher's *dialectical process* by saying that it was not something to picture but that it was a matter, solely, of thinking this idea as process. When the student complained that this was far too abstract, he replied, 'The dialectical process is very concrete, by contrast to that washerwoman there' — pointing to a woman in a courtyard — 'who only figures in your mind in an abstract and indeterminate way.'

Some cinema enthusiasts in the early period referred to the deadening nature of the literate, text-oriented mind and its verbalized remarks. They sought the 'living', pictorial human mind not so much in words as in a person's face and gestural movements. Even if it is understandable that people were weary of an intellectualism at one remove from experience, and its hollow or academic phrases, it is equally clear why these 'redemptive' perspectives, formulated into a programme by cinema enthusiasts in the brief period of the silent movie, remained entirely ineffectual. Talkies strikingly showed that they too could produce thoughtless phrases and primitive hubbub. At any rate, cinema was not alone in manifesting the 'visible spirit' that people sought to conjure.

> The invention of the art of printing gradually rendered the human face indecipherable. The visible spirit became a legible one, and visual culture, conceptual. But the cinematographer gives culture a new impulse towards the visual, and the human

being a new countenance. The human face has become our expressive canvas. (Balázs)

Spoken language alienates the human being from the reality of things and from himself. (Ibid)

All Expressionist artists have been struggling for years for this kind of new, living and archetypal communication of gesture. That is why the bioscope is one of the characteristic discoveries in the artistic field. (Gerhard Hauptmann, German playwright)

From Aeschylus and Euripides onwards, all poets have cursed language. If it now proves possible to reproduce a wordless poetry wordlessly [i.e. in silent film], can such an art be surpassed? The cinema is the culminating perfection of four millennia of poetry. (Yahu, Japanese writer)

But let us now leave the field where personal predilections, dressed up as opinions, clash with one another, and where different thoughts collide. In this domain it would be impossible to understand the intentions that Rudolf Steiner associated with the art of film.

5

Rudolf Steiner, in a lecture on 27 February 1917 in Berlin

A particularly fine means of chasing people into materialism is
something scarcely perceived from this perspective: the cinema
and film. There is no better means to inculcate materialism than
through film. You see, what we apprehend in a film is not reality
as human beings see it. Only an era that has so little idea of
reality that it worships reality as idol in the form of materialism,
can believe that film offers reality. Ask yourself honestly:
what you have seen on the street — is it actually closer to an
unmoving picture made by a painter or the dreadful twinkling
image of the cinematic film? What the cinematographer offers
people hunkers down in a deeper material stratum than what
we otherwise have in sense perception. Etherically we become
saucer-eyed. And here an effect is exerted not only upon what
resides in our conscious mind but a materializing effect is
exerted on our deepest subconscious. Please do not take this
as a polemic against film. It must again be expressly stated that
cinematography is a natural and inevitable development. The
art of cinematography will develop more and more, and this will
be the path into materialism. A counterweight must be created,
and this can only involve combining the reality addiction as
developed in cinema with something else. Just as we here
develop an addictive descent below sensory perception, so at the
same time we must ascend above sensory perception or in other
words develop upward into the world of spirit. Then film will
not harm us however much we view cinematic images.

In referring here to a 'deeper material stratum', Steiner is addressing
the action of film images on the body. The anti-organic foundations
of media-induced perception prevent our inner, conscious aspect,
from connecting with the content of perception; in fact the latter

repels it. In consequence, a hardening action is exerted on the life or etheric body — which is the lowest supersensibly active organization which pervades the physical body as mediator of life processes such as growth, breathing, nutrition, warmth-suffusion, reproduction etc. In reductive science, its manifest sensory forms of expression are described as physiological, chemical and biological hybrid processes, to which life-sustaining capacities are ascribed.

When he speaks of people becoming 'etherically saucer-eyed' he means the paralysis and deadening of soul constituents involved in the visual process. Goethe emphatically refers to this in his *Theory of Colours*. There he describes how each colour is in interplay with what he called 'sensory-moral' sense perception. (In the 'moral' aspect which the recipient of a visual stimulus adds to optical experience, there manifests what was described in the previous chapter as the ideal, spiritual completion of a sense impression.)

Deadening of optical perception arose in cinematography due to the fact that viewers, while inside the 'black box', stared for over a third of the time into pitch dark, unconsciously and unsuccessfully trying to experience the cinematographic simulation of perception in a way as inwardly ensouled (sensory-moral) as in unhindered sense perception. This is impossible given the frantic, anti-organic stroboscopic bombardment at a rate of 24 images per second. The rotating Maltese Cross — this also, by the way, invented by a Berliner — at the same time marked the phases of darkness in which the picture transfer occurred.

Modern digital image relay retained the 24 frames per second. Now, though, there is no longer a phase of darkness since the single images are 'written' additively, mostly in successive half-images, at unimaginable speed in a lineal script consisting of quadratic pixels. In this process, the 'distraction' expected by film viewers is initiated to a degree greater than they ought to want, in subconscious depths of their sense physiology.

Thus we have purchased the apparent vitality of moving film figures at the cost of a subtly-dosed deadening of perception through media technology. In a different context Rudolf Steiner pointed out that the vigour of the ancient Greeks' sense organization far surpassed what we possess today, and that they would scarcely have survived several hours of watching a film, though assuredly passing out before it took dire effect.

Addiction to a reality surrogate procures for viewers their typical release from a daily life experienced as poor in entertainment value. The sense of being entertained, in the majority of visual media, is based on a general cultural failing. Since people have not yet learned how to activate and grasp hold of inner spiritual formative forces, they compensate for this vacuum through technical, ready-made imaginations. And thus a veil continues to be drawn over what would, if seen clearly, no longer hold any fascination for them.

Media entertainment nowadays takes place only to a small degree in the classical cinema, where, around the turn of the nineteenth to the twentieth century, media first marched into human consciousness. Today this has expanded to the countless small-scale image-surfaces of laptops, tablets and smartphones, advertising panels and home cinemas, TV and DVD-player screens. Technical advances to satisfy the materialistic addiction to reality by adding the third dimension, and shifting it into interactive gaming, above all in the erotic, sex and video game industry by the use of V(irtual) R(eality) headsets, will be driven forward in future not least because of the gigantic new sources of income they offer.

Filmmakers, most of whom see few films apart from their own, have very varied professional motivations. One of the great innovators of 'film language', Jean-Luc Godard, said this: '[cinematic] depiction consoles us for the sadness of life. Life consoles us for the fact that depiction is nothing.' Yet, in the vicious circle of his consolations, Jean-Luc Godard remains on very shaky ground: for life is not necessarily sadder without the cinema, nor are the images with which cinema entertains us nothing. After all, they greatly influence both our thinking and our behaviour.

An ardent cinema-lover, who worked as a mask maker in numerous Berlin film productions, admitted to me that he drew on his cinematic experience at decisive moments of his life: for instance at a job interview, on his first date, at a time of urban isolation and similar. Recalling a film star in a comparable situation, he said, provided a script for his 'role' in each case, was a model he could imitate in the so-called 'real world' so as to behave in socially acceptable ways. By contrast I had sought to test cinema's capacity as an expressive medium. In the case of this film fan I encountered the uncomfortable fact that the cinema's reflected world of illusion had begun to rebound psychologically and morally on 'real' life.

My video sura, *Vom Guten Bild* ('The Good Picture') contains six lines of fading-in text dedicated to 'good' pictorial illusion:[16] 1) 'I created the world from being and nothingness'; 2) 'I created it so that it might appear to you'; 3) Appearance is good if you glimpse my light within it'; 4) 'It becomes evil if you lose your heart to its images'; 5) 'The image of appearance lapses from reality'; 6) 'It succumbs to the void'.

This short experimental film gave expression to the concern that we ought not to sacrifice our ability to distinguish reality and appearance, essence and phenomenon, to the miasma of a consumerist dream. It was to serve as a reminder that ultimately the life processes within the viewer's organ of sight were what elicited the after-images in the cinema auditorium; and that, through the subconscious, successive fusion of each image flashing on the retina, movement pictures were invoked which endowed the screen schemas with a seemingly intrinsic life, though in reality one concealed from the viewer. In my novel, *Hieronymus — on Cinema and Love in Eras of Reincarnation*, it would be difficult to disagree with the protagonist, a disillusioned film maker, in his conclusion that 'Film and television are the high priests of the doctrine that life arises from death. But they can only impart life to their lemurs by sucking it out of their viewers.'

In a general discussion about the medium of cinema following the filming of his *The Never-Ending Story*, which he found so unsatisfactory,[17] Michael Ende suggested that Rudolf Steiner would have changed his views if he had known about modern, more advanced media techniques. Since I am familiar with Steiner's accounts and prophecies in many realms of life, and their far-reaching significance for the future, I have good reason to doubt

Michael Ende's conjecture. On the contrary, I am convinced that in Steiner's comment that 'The art of cinematography will develop more and more', he was intimating forms of visual media that go beyond advances in film technology that even Michael Ende, in his later era, was aware of. From Virtual Reality headsets through image transmitters directly implanted in the brain, we can now envisage further stages on the path to dependency upon dead images. 'This will be the path into materialism', remarked Steiner, referring not only to materialist intellectualism but also to a resulting deadening of the individual's shaping imagination.

Yet Steiner never urged the abolition of film. Rather, with his insight into the spiritual origins of film technology's development, he *characterized* its potential to consolidate the ahrimanic influence[18] and to cultivate a humanity blind to knowledge and therefore also to reality, saying that for this very reason it would have a great future.

Rudolf Steiner in Stuttgart, 11 July 1923

...Please do not take the negative things I say negatively. I don't want to take anything away from modern culture. The more things are developed, the more enthusiasm I have for them. I don't want to get rid of either telegraphy or cinema — such a thing would never occur to me.[19] But it is really necessary to consider that two things oppose each other everywhere. The world is entirely taken up with externalization. And just as one has to dry oneself after taking a bath so the balance must be redressed by immersing oneself in the spirit if, by contrast, a culture of outward tangibility is continually increasing. It is precisely this that will prompt us to become all the more active: being externally caught up in things that no longer work through us but work upon us so that we ourselves are excluded as soul and spirit...

With somewhat different emphasis, Rudolf Steiner expressed in Stuttgart what he had already said in Berlin. Full self-awareness, he said, involved the will for inner observation of our own part in the emergence of ideas and thoughts, of feelings and will impulses.

By perceiving subconscious premises of our mind's workings, this observation at the same time secures the free scope for original, truly human action. This will for soul attentiveness, serving inner elucidation, can neither be developed nor sustained in the cinema or in front of a computer screen.

This encapsulates the great responsibility of the visual entertainment industry, whose media producers show little inclination to be cognisant of it. Governed by crass, albeit popular psychological models such as the Behaviourism we have been discussing, they seek to exert an undiluted influence on their viewers' thoughts and emotions. Even if motivated by the ideal of offering cinema-goers only the 'best entertainment', they still cannot avoid playing their part in a general weakening of human powers of awareness.

A viewer who, as he sits in the cinema, does not remain conscious of his humanity (as a thinking, striving and possibly despairing and self-confronting being) will not bring any understanding to bear on the spiritually real figuration and destiny-revealing trajectory of the film he is watching. And since the film industry never embarks on uncalculated risks but makes sure that, by investing ever larger sums, it secures its advantage in the world of marketing propaganda, it regards itself as compelled to choose a form of 'visual entertainment' that directly addresses the thirst for effortless stimulation and diffuse 'distraction'.

Sometimes, it is true, one finds depicted in the qualities and attributes of film heroes instances of great selflessness and loving devotion, or other exemplary virtues. Yet when these qualities figure in feel-good films of love and drama they are rarely carefully drawn nor is their developmental trajectory really depicted. The hero becomes, perhaps, the near-caricature of someone faithful unto death (say in *Cold Mountain*), the heroine a figure who battles for justice against all odds (as in *Erin Brockovich*). No light is shone on the origins of these heroic moral powers, and therefore they seem simply to have fallen from heaven. Thus their poignancy is illusory.

The majority of films are however founded on a fascination with cunning psychopaths: monsters leaping fully-formed from the screen-plays of famous directors such as Lars von Trier, Quentin

Tarantino, Tim Burton, Michael Haneke, Ridley Scott et al. These films help titillate an interest in grotesquely inhuman figures and their criminal careers without disturbing the entertainment thrill of their audiences through any sharper evaluation than a subjective mix of feelings and horror. 'It's only cinema', will say those who have so far declined to scrutinize what cinema actually is.

Every thought and every feeling allows what we may call an 'elemental' to arise in our mental-spiritual space,[20] and thereafter to lead a life independent of its originator, albeit with the tendency to relate back to the latter in future from without. The moral miasma of elementals engendered in media consumption (whether this be in the film genres of sex, horror, love kitsch or end-time hysteria) accumulates energy through the number of consumers, gradually erasing consciousness of the boundary separating inner from outer. In addition, this makes it easier to overleap unnoticed actual levels of appearance and reality. The technique used in many forms of occultism of erasing levels of reality is employed, for instance, in apocalyptic visions of science-fiction fantasy, of catastrophic end-time myths or extraterrestrial idylls. Future visions of civilization are thus repeatedly depicted in bombastic and suggestive images that subconsciously smooth the way for their realization.

That production of a media power founded on psychological assault can sometimes come back to haunt the mental state of those chiefly responsible for it at the western dream factory's Californian hub, has only recently come to public attention, even though accusations of sexual molestation, rape and criminal paedophilia circles have always been voiced by victims who broke the terrible silence. Marilyn Monroe, already, wrote this in her memoir *My Story*:

> The big film bosses were closer to the film business than anyone else. So you sat with them and listened to their lies and manipulation. And you saw Hollywood with their eyes — a cram-packed brothel.

The leading film and pop music periodical *Variety* stated that 'abuse is engrained in the DNA of the entertainment industry'.[21] It is beyond the scope of this book to examine why it is only now, after countless out-of-court settlements, that a case is being brought against one of the most successful film producers in Hollywood.[22]

Though somewhat out of sight and public scrutiny, dubious 'forms of entertainment' that offer an addictively intensified reality, and now figure on the porn internet and game consoles, have come to be a hugely lucrative field worth several times that of 'normal' film production.[23] In future years this phenomenon will necessitate withdrawal strategies and therapies on a global scale, as in other areas of medically diagnosed addiction.[24] Already before the flood-gates opened with the internet, documented forms of social breakdown-related cinema addiction had developed in big cities, with addicts feeling compelled to go to the cinema several times every day for many years.[25]

Very generally, in the film context, we need to seek the 'counterweight to the reality addiction', that Steiner urged, on two levels: firstly in the field of photographic technology and reproduction, and secondly in the sphere of filmic imagination. As opposed to a predetermined dramatic narrative, the latter must create connections both between single shots and settings, and between these and the auditory realm.[26]

A future 'spirit of film'[27] can be characterized by saying that it will not sedate but activate the ideas and I consciousness of film recipients, who will retain higher levels of complete reality in their awareness.

This must be supported by a technical configuration of the sphere of perception that does not overburden the 'etheric life forces'.[28] For this purpose, physiological processes must be treated in a technically 'softer' way than occurs in one-sided efforts to establish 3-D cinema. Some aspects of this are described in my novel, *Hieronymus — on Cinema and Love in Eras of Reincarnation*, for instance the 'water screen',[29] the technique for eliminating fade-to-blacks, and the temporal extending of individual images to the point of discernibility, as was the case at the beginning of film. The latter would mean relinquishing the full illusion of motion. In connection with this the strengths of the black-and-white image and the light control that it facilitates could be recalled,[30] perhaps also entirely dispensing with 3-D simulation and the blending of computer-generated forms with real actors. Image snippets at the boundaries of perception, much used in adverts and music videos, are also unworthy of a human state of consciousness. It can be hoped that further technical inventions will be made, and above all implemented, which would serve to relieve physiological burdens on the viewer's visual process, and thus could create further potential for experiencing spiritual forces of configuration in future art films.

The only film director I know of who (apart from me) has described the underlying tendency of film technology to favour materialistic amorality through authoritarian consumer compulsion, was Pier Paolo Pasolini. He said this:

> All irrational, oneiric, primitive and barbaric moments in film are kept below the level of consciousness, and exploited to influence and manipulate. And around this hypnotic monster that a film invariably is, people have quickly built the narrative convention that has provided the material for superfluous and pseudo-critical comparisons with theatre and the novel. [31]

And:

> I repeat: It is important that I acknowledge this aversion within me to mere utilitarian use of consumer goods. The antipathy I feel within me is so unendurably strong that I cannot fix my eyes for more than a few moments on a TV screen. This is a physical reaction: disgust overcomes me. In fact, the whole of consumer culture irritates me. [32]

6

In 1983, readers of the monthly journal *Info3* (based in Frankfurt, Germany) were offered a sequence of articles in several successive issues about the artistic potential of the cinema and its limitations, in response to an essay on this theme by Michael Ende. As mentioned previously, Ende was writing here about the filming of his best-seller, *The Never-Ending Story*, which had left him highly dissatisfied. (Conflict with the film producer reached such a level that he was even barred from the film set.) In his essay he sought dialogue with other authors, and with the readers of a journal regarded as 'anthroposophical'.

In this context, some of the critical remarks about the cinema by Steiner that we have already cited were aired, relativized by Ende in so far as Steiner could only have seen very technically imperfect films (I have already commented on this). Ende sought the reasons for Steiner's cinema critique in other factors, though what these were was not clear to him. At the point when a response to these articles was drying up, a reader's letter from J.E. Zeylmans van Emmichoven was published.[33] He is well known in anthroposophic circles as priest and author of a four-volume biography of Ita Wegman, an important physician and close collaborator with Rudolf Steiner. At least until the moment when his letter was published, his credibility was beyond doubt. The letter, published in the April 1983 issue of *Info3*, ran as follows:

> Michael Ende says that Rudolf Steiner was opposed to cinema, and that he even has evidence of comments to that effect by Dr Steiner. I would therefore like to put it on record that, curiously, I can testify to the opposite. For five years I was secretary to the Dutch publisher Pieter de Haan, who joined the Society in 1912, and, until 1924 had many conversations with Rudolf Steiner. Thus he had a very close acquaintance with him. Mr de Haan

often told me that Dr Steiner wanted us to make films. According
to de Haan, Rudolf Steiner said that it was a suitable medium
for presenting the laws of destiny in the course of recurring
incarnations. It is my belief that Dr Steiner was a little different
from how many nowadays imagine him to have been.

This message had no great impact on students of anthroposophy
who, conversant with the dangers of unreflective use of technical
media such as the phonograph and cinematograph — to which
Steiner had expressly referred — did not find access to the deeper-
reaching artistic impulse that necessarily proceeds precisely from
overcoming conditions that render spiritual apprehension more
difficult. And yet this social impulse of aesthetic and therapeutic
transformation was what primarily governed Rudolf Steiner's
responses to all phenomena of life. When for example, in a lecture
given in Wales, he stated how easy it was, in that special place,
to develop imaginative perception associated with a productive
pictorial thinking, and that this singularity was attributable at the
time to the relative lack of car traffic in the region, he nevertheless
took care to avoid preconceptions by adding the following remark:

> I am not saying anything against cars, as I mentioned already.
> Anthroposophy cannot be reactionary. Naturally I myself take
> great pleasure in driving in a car if it's necessary. We can't try to
> turn the clock back. No, but we must seek to balance whatever
> arises with its opposite, and then travelling by car will be entirely
> right. Yet alongside car travel, and everything associated with it,
> must arise a heart that is inclined to the world of spirit. And then,
> whatever other things also come beside car travel, humanity will
> be able to imbue itself ... with its own necessary strength and
> freedom.[34]

Thus Rudolf Steiner also, for instance, referred to the injurious
effect on the heart of typewriting as was common then, using machines that hammered each separate letter onto paper. Elsewhere
he spoke of the deadening effect on self-awareness of induction
currents that were associated at the time with increasing electricity
cables. Here too he was a hundred years ahead of his time in

understanding the electro-smog phenomenon. In addition, he forecast a third energy source that would appear in the near future alongside electricity and magnetism. Though he did not name atomic energy as such, he hoped that by the time it was discovered humanity would have achieved the necessary moral progress by studying spiritual science, since otherwise use of this technology would lead to the complete collapse of human civilization.

Steiner's prophetic acuity, which proved itself in various other fields, has since been noted with astonishment and acknowledgement by those aware of such matters (he referred, for instance, to phenomena of decline in public healthcare, factory farming,[35] in the disappearance of trees and medicinal herbs, and in the emergence of new epidemic diseases).

There is a qualitative difference between inventions of practical utility such as trains or industrial production machines — for which he himself offered significant research stimulus — and those that connect with our feeling and desire nature. In just one of his lectures, he referred to the gramophone, the technically primitive forerunner of the headset and thus of the ear-wired addiction of our own times. He showed a good deal of concern about this invention in the lecture already referred to in Penmaenmawr (Wales):

> Forgive me for ending on this seemingly trivial note, but things are different in the case of the gramophone. Here humanity tries to force art into the mechanical element. And if humanity were to develop a passionate preference for such things, mechanizing what descends into the world as the shadow of the spiritual, if humanity therefore developed enthusiasm for things such as the gramophone, then it could no longer defend itself against them. The gods would have to help. Well, the gods are merciful, and as yet we can still hope that, as human civilization advances, the merciful gods will help us further to overcome aberrations of taste such as those expressed in the gramophone.

In relation to cinema, he wanted to see insightful film-makers — who, as the letter from Emmichoven testifies — develop types of film that avoid manipulative use of visual media in order to narrate fantastical, 'non-human' stories. Thus he was hoping presumably not only for new content in film, but for new types of audience and target groups when he spoke to the energetic publisher and entrepreneur Pieter de Haan about film as a 'suitable medium for presenting the laws of destiny in the course of recurring incarnations'.

A film liberated from the materialistic caricature of the human being cannot be programmatically released into the world, but is associated with newly developing capacities of filmic portrayal and narrative. Likewise it requires new forms of production and dissemination, as well as appropriate, and necessarily 'risk-intensive' funding invested in artistic innovations. It presupposes film producers inspired to bring about deep-seated change in the field of cinema. From my own experience I know how great are the hindrances currently mustered against realization of such developments.

Between 2003 and 2005, I made preparations at various levels for realizing a film project whose reincarnation theme had been proposed back in 1973 — thus 30 years earlier — to the Swiss Film Funding Department. The film project carried the unusually long working title of *You don't step twice in the same river or After me will come the one who was before me.*[36] On 22 June 1973, Swiss Federal Council member Hanspeter Tschudi — at that time chairman of the Film Promotion Department — personally sent the following message to explain why the project had been turned down:

> The screenplay project *You don't step twice in the same river or After me will come the one who was before me* is convincing neither in thematic nor artistic terms. The theme seems confused, and the message of the film remains unclear. Ultimately the intention is scarcely comprehensible.

At a young age, already, it seemed to me that it would be well worth the time and money to present images of successive lives on earth; and so Zeylmans van Emmichoven's letter about Rudolf Steiner's intentions for film in April 1983 struck me like a bolt of lightning. As early as June 1983, this moved me to give a lecture entitled 'The Mediumistic Nature of Cinema', and at the subsequent discussion I spoke about the recently published *Info3* letter and discussed it with the audience.[37]

Thirty years later, I took up this film project once again, which led to a sequence of six film scripts, and trips to all planned shoots in Berlin, the tri-region area (where France, Switzerland and Baden-Württemberg meet) and the Pyrenees. During the trips we already secured film-shoot permits for some of these locations. Preparatory negotiations were held with a Swiss and a German film producer, most of the actors were chosen, and, in the summer of 2004 a one-week workshop on the penultimate screenplay script was held for the actors and camerawoman. Yet this second attempt to create a serious film on the theme of reincarnation likewise faltered by the end of 2005.[38] Forty years after the first film treatment, the screenplay metamorphosed, at least, into literary form in the novel *Hieronymus – on Cinema and Love in Eras of Reincarnation*, and was published in 2013.[39]

In a review of the Hieronymus novel for *Gegenwart* (Bern), Markus Sieber cited the letter in *Info3* written by Zeylmans van Emmichoven. In the next issue of *Gegenwart*, a repudiation appeared as follows: 'This citation published in *Info3* (April 1983) cannot be right as it stands, since there are a wealth of other diametrically opposed statements [by Steiner]. What Rudolf Steiner may have said is this: We should seek alternatives to the cinema.'[40] The person thus casting doubt on the letter then referred to a statement by Steiner about the initiative he had taken up with Jan Stuten for an 'alternative to the cinema'. In the author's view this could have been the only objective seriously pursued by Steiner in this field.

Before we come to speak of Steiner's intentions for a 'reincarnation film' that would accord with reality, I will briefly mention the remarkable initiative by Jan Stuten, and Rudolf Steiner's support for it. Here we will see a further example of Steiner's great capacity to stimulate and support innovative artistic impulses. But we must avoid thinking that Steiner here sought a 'substitute' for the cinema, as a contemporary phenomenon that should be avoided or even combated. After all, aware of the tendency in his listeners to keep problematic cultural influences at arm's length, he had repeatedly stated this: '...Please do not take the negative things I say negatively... I don't want to get rid of ... cinema — such a thing would never occur to me.' (See quotation on p. 26.)

7

Jan Stuten (1890–1948)

Jan Stuten (1890–1948) was a musician, a composer for numerous stage works, a painter, architect and set designer, and besides this was chosen by Rudolf Steiner to be the first actor to play Faust in the production staged by Marie Steiner. Certainly he was an individual who keenly embraced the idea of the 'total artwork'. In particular he sought innovation when commissioned to design the lighting for eurythmy and theatre performances, and Steiner supported him in this. At the end of the First World War, in the autumn of 1918, Steiner himself approached him to suggest that he investigate the possibilities of a new 'light-show art' as he called it.* In a conversation reproduced in one of the comprehensive documentations of this shared initiative,[41] Steiner said that film was a coming art form of great importance since it met an elementary need of people — their hunger for a world of images — in a sophisticated way. Yet he called film inartistic because it was 'unmusical'. The musical interval, he said, involves the listener accomplishing an inner transition from one tone to another, whereas there was nothing at

---

* Translator's note: 'Licht-Spiel' (literally 'light play') is a term still used today to refer to cinema and film.

all equivalent in film. This is a far-reaching verdict if we consider that it is precisely in the intervals, thus the spaces and transitions in sensory data, that a spiritual content finds entry into an artwork.

Steiner was seeking to place alongside the 'powerfully emerging new medium' something that 'employed similar means but is directly configured by the human being and not supplied ready-made by a separate, technical apparatus'. When Stuten asked him for a specific theme, Steiner recommended that of 'fear'.

Under Steiner's direction, the Goetheanum stage, also in matters of lighting — especially of eurythmy movement sequences — had taken innovative paths that were then taken up by other theatres and lighting designers. Wieland and Wolfgang Wagner, for instance, in the 'wonder of the new Bayreuth' from 1950 onward, simplified and clarified the staging of illumined stage props originally envisaged by Richard Wagner. There is no scope here to describe in detail the technical stage developments conceived by Jan Stuten, his son Christian Stuten, and the inventor and physician Hans Jenny for specific performances at the Goetheanum overseen by director Wilfried Hammacher (born 1928).[42] It is enough to know that new, enlarged and expanded means of lighting were tested, that could configure qualitatively different spaces which transform and interpenetrate, or collapse back into black.

To give a single example, one light arrangement, which Hans Jenny called a 'basic light plan', was the following: a blue and a red light shine upon a back wall or gauze, which becomes violet in colour. When a form, for instance a circle, is held before the red beam, its shadow appears blue on the backdrop, and vice versa. A form deviating from the first form, but still corresponding to it — such as a ring — can also of course be held up in front of the blue beam, and will then appear as a red ring around the blue circle.

But now the colour modulation becomes richer by engendering coloured shadows. If a blue light source casts a shadow from the circle raised into the beam, the shadow naturally appears black. But if the black shadow is illumined by a second, white light, the shadow does not brighten to a grey or light grey but wonderfully becomes the complementary colour to blue — orange.

And if the shadows, for instance by means of skilful hands, are now set in motion and assume either diffuse or sharply outlined forms, and thus if several different light sources are configured by different people, a whole lighting orchestra arises, especially if additional gauzes, back projections and transparencies are employed. In the essay referred to in the journal *Bühnentechnische Rundschau*, Hans Jenny writes as follows about a lighting sequence in Shakespeare's *The Tempest*, produced in 1966/68:

> Through the form-play of hands, the whole strikes one as a fresh and ad hoc creation, non-mechanical and concretized in new, innovative kinds of dimension. There is nothing reminiscent of a painted or mechanical staging of water, wind etc. Fourteen people formed, as it were, the lighting orchestra, and played upon their light sources in accord with the colour libretto. As with any orchestra, practice and rehearsal were much needed; and since everything was being tried out for the first time, it was not only a question of creating harmony but also of acquiring the necessary hand skills.

Employing the synaesthetic effects of 'auditory light' and 'visible music', Rudolf Steiner wanted to inform stage art with a large-scale sculpting of colour space. Those who have witnessed these kinds of experiments in large symphonic eurythmy performances will not forget the incomparable effect of a breathing and pulsing 'total space' configured and structured in fields of colour. This seems to draw one's feelings into the stage area, enabling the watcher as it were to 'dream along' in an active yet self-oblivious way with the spiritual forces of configuration that infuse and flash through the space. By comparison with this, technically demanding and illusion-promoting 3-D film technology creates a forcible isolation within one's own head. In April 2013 I was a guest invited to the premiere of the blockbuster *Star Trek Into Darkness*, at the CineStar Cinema in Berlin's Sony Centre.

Director Abrams was on a promotional tour with his whole film crew. This excessively long space-war film was showing simultaneously in several auditoria. Although a large crowd was

The author at the German premiere of Star Trek Into Darkness *in Berlin*

in attendance, there was no sense of a shared artistic experience. Instead the atmosphere was one of a group brain-washing endurance session dressed up as entertainment. The fantastically absurd story did what it could to ensure that its viewers forgot not only that their experience was one mediated solely by the sense apparatus of the head but also that they possessed a whole, terribly neglected, living body with its breathing and blood circulation, and equipped with limbs. Suffering from a virtually created locked-in syndrome, the viewers' independent power of thinking was so greatly impaired that it was well-nigh impossible — or at least it seemed superfluous — for them to develop a residual sense that they might consciously reflect on the externally induced sensory and subsensory experience they were having. The endlessly drawn out, cataleptic world-destruction became increasingly unreal and unbearably pointless to me. Afterwards, viewers trudged past the security staff like zombies, and stumbled into the open air. This 3-D spectacle left its viewers speechless and dumb-struck. The pleasure of watching a film with other people, and the enjoyment of discussing it with them afterwards is, on the other hand, a cultural value to which a future, spiritually concretized film must remain faithful.

But back now to Stuten's light-play project. Several playwrights of recent decades have used their stage directions to more or less urge an expansion of lighting techniques. Rudolf Steiner does something similar when he gives the following instruction for one of his plays: 'A space not limited by artificial walls but by tree-like, interwoven plants and forms that expand and send runners and offshoots into the interior. The whole is in turbulent motion and sometimes filled with storm.' (*The Guardian of the Threshold*, Scene 6).

Or here is Albert Steffen, too, in his stage directions for The Manichaeans, for which Hans Jenny was lighting director when it was performed in the 60s: 'A green, rising slope. The furthest peaks are ringed by the Manichaeans. Their ranks look like a golden ring that shines powerfully forth. Above, a cloudless sky. Below, dark moorland, with mist rolling over it.' (Act 1).

As in all artistic processes in which Steiner was involved, he always considered various ideas and left things open initially in conversations with Jan Stuten, not predetermining them: dancers? Puppets? Shadow-play? Actors? He referred, for instance, to old shadow-theatre traditions that he said Stuten should find out about.

As far as the theme of 'fear' is concerned, it is not by chance that Robert Wiene shot the film *Furcht* ('Fear') in Berlin in 1917. The film was first shown on 21 September in Berlin's Mozart Hall. Since Rudolf Steiner had been in Berlin throughout that September, it is certainly possible that he was present at one of the showings. We can recall here a comment by Herbert Hahn — 'He went to the cinema from time to time to see especially typical and characteristic new films.'

Wiene's film *Furcht* seeks to create tension by its focus on spirit hauntings. A young, aristocratic globetrotter and art collector takes wrongful possession of a Buddha statue in India. At home in Berlin he is increasingly plagued by insomnia. A demon who protects the statue gradually drives him mad, and the film ends with the young man's suicide. Two years later, Wiese shot the highly successful film *The Cabinet of Dr Caligari* at Babelsberger Studios. For the first time, this raised German film to world status and established the Expressionist silent-movie film tradition of figures such as Lang (*Dr Mabuse*, 1922, *Metropolis*, 1927) and Murnau (*Nosferatu*, 1922, *Faust* 1926).

Jan Stuten took up the theme of 'Fear' and initially drafted a series of 15 colour sketches, conceived as staging guidelines, which show the metamorphosis of an intensifying fear through death and resurrection until it is overcome in a peacefully illumined world.[43] He began at the same time to draft musical compositions for each picture or scene. The middle one, the eighth, for example, was shaped by the 'hectic, driving, staccato drum-kit beat of jazz'.

Stuten also wrote: 'The last pictures are only hints; here the movement of colours is entirely governed by the music, whereas in the first half the music is conceived as being more influenced by the image. This initial draft sequence was sketched in 1918.' Thus we find here an aesthetically pleasing development sequence in which the dominance of vision (in the phase of fear) is gradually ceded to hearing, as fear is dispelled. This can remind us of the famous Aristotelian definition of Tragedy, about which Rudolf Steiner said the following in his lecture on 13 May 1921:

> Into the sentient soul, through which surged our drives, desires and passions, the powers governing earthly evolution allow something to flow that is very wholesome for the human being, and without which he could not form the right relationship to his surroundings. That is, <u>fear</u>. Without fear a person would feel intimate with everything of a higher nature, and would seek to bear the democracy inscribed upon earth into the worlds of spirit. When he opposes fear with his I in the right way, he transforms it into reverence, into piety... Nowadays people are so averse to awakening a fear of ghosts in children. If this is taken too far it is harmful, but it does no harm for children to have a sense that something holds sway behind the visible world. Children who have never met this feeling through fairytales find it much harder to develop a sense of reverence; and adults' fear of children's fear of ghosts is really quite unnecessary.

The proposed theme has little to do with the suggestiveness of horror films, since they never show fear overcome: the unconstrained action of this emotion is the intrinsic basis of such films' imprisoning effect on the viewer, which these films seek to elicit. After Rudolf Steiner's death (1925), Stuten pursued his suggestions further until his own premature death in 1949. At the Paris World Exhibition in 1938, The *Faust* production from Dornach's Goetheanum stage, with stage design and music by Jan Stuten, met with great international acclaim. The American team around Walt Disney showed parti-cular interest in eurythmy. Some of his colleagues sought out Stuten and had him explain to them this new art of movement that Rudolf Steiner had created, which called itself 'visible music' and 'visible speech'. At this World Exhibition, too, Stuten himself had made enquiries into the latest developments in projection and lighting technique. The film people around Disney also studied Stuten's 15 sketches on 'The Metamorphoses of Fear' with great interest.

In 1940, Disney's film *Fantasia* appeared, with its orchestral performances of several world-famous works of classical music including a toccata by Bach, Schubert's *Ave Verum* and Mussorgsky's *Night on Bald Mountain*. Rudolf Kutzli was struck by the curious affinity between the film and the movement language of eurythmy, and had several conversations with Stuten during which the connection came to light, as we described. Though lit in unusually strong colour, Disney's film starts 'naturalistically', but soon resorts to the tools of the animated cartoon genre of the day. Kutzli commented as follows:

> As the cello began to play, the instrument shone out in a warm red, while the flute tones appeared as bright yellow rays... The musicians transform themselves mysteriously. The outer gradually fading to become a play of moving coloured shadows, changing forms, visible music, visible song. The images accom-panying the Bach Fugue are assuredly inspired by the Stuten sketches, in fact almost even directly copied from them at times. *Fantasia*, with the fear motif that Rudolf Steiner had recommended to Stuten twenty years previously, here became a perfect antagonist to Rudolf Steiner's intentions.

The irony of fate: the Hollywood dream factory scores a global success with *Fantasia*, while the initiative of Steiner pursued by Stuten is relegated to complete oblivion.[44] Or, as an Italian proverb puts it, 'When good Christians try to build a chapel somewhere, the devil has long since built his cathedral there.'

Given my previous thoughts here, it will be clear that I do not see the Rudolf Steiner-Walt Disney opposition as a primitive good and evil dualism, but rather as two opposing aesthetic approaches and conditions. The one urges artistically sustained communication requiring active powers of imagination and thinking, while the other overwhelms the recipient with an only apparent, but in fact complete lack, of communication.

Supported by colleagues like Stuten, and later Hans Jenny, Steiner sought to use the most modern stage design methods to create theatre in which a community of people could have both a sensory and soul experience of spatial dimensions created by coloured light and shadows. Some prominent lighting designers have taken up these efforts again and developed them further — people ranging from the Adolphe Appia in Switzerland from 1900 onwards, to the Englishman Robert Wilson.

I have presented Rudolf Steiner's approach to the related field of stage design and dramatic art, and his innovative ideas in stage technology, in order to show how untenable it is to think that he would have shied away from using film if he had been presented with an opportunity to shape it as he wished.

8

At this point I want to return to the key issue that I have already raised. Can Rudolf Steiner — and, as we have heard, some of his followers dispute this — really have suggested creating films that draw their content from scientific enquiries into the world of spirit yet at the same time avoid sliding into a kind of 'doctrinal' film experience? Could he have proposed a form of cinema whose authors strive to attain an independent capacity of unprejudiced judgement, and thus render themselves able to contribute to such an art of film? Below I will explain my reasons for answering this question in the affirmative.

Let us recall, firstly, that everything seems to depend here on the credibility of the reader's letter in *Info3* (April 1983) (see p. 31f.). To explore what was needed for a film production, Steiner repeatedly discussed this with Pieter de Haan, who struck him as a possible producer for it. He was aware that funding would be far from a minor aspect in creating a film that sought public regard. In 1920 there was, of course, no one within the anthroposophic movement who had specific knowledge of film-making. Even outside the movement there were no established filmmaking institutions in Germany at the time. Only when he had become aware of several people who were willing and able to get involved, did his conviction that film was a 'suitable medium for presenting the laws of destiny in the course of recurring incarnations' start to figure for him in terms of possible artistic cinematic realization.

Rudolf Steiner was the first dramatist in the world to present the development of characters through several earthly lives in a sequence of plays, and thus to open up a new, historically and culturally important dimension in European theatrical tradition. Though completion of his cycle of plays was prevented by the outbreak of the First World War — he had planned seven plays

— performance of the existing four is associated with difficulties scarcely manageable within mainstream theatre. Despite this, they give expression to an epic change in knowledge and consciousness, founded on Rudolf Steiner's spiritual-scientific insights into the human being and the world and his incorporation of the reality of supersensible spheres. If I try to imagine what would have arisen if Steiner had become creatively involved in film — he was of course, by his own testimony, involved with it as a viewer — the following suggests itself:

1. His analysis of the dulling and passivity-intensifying effect on the viewer of movement simulation does not diminish the innovative nature of themes that he suggested for a film. The 'etheric saucer-eyes' effect applies also to a film that deals with destiny and reincarnation.

2. If there are general, fundamental laws for aesthetics, then they apply also to the art of film. That is, it must develop shaping ideas, imaginative (naturalistic) expressive values in a way that is apt for its material, and is neither symbolic nor allegorical. As we know, decades passed after the invention of cinema before filmmakers such as Godard, Antonioni, Fellini, Tarkovsky et al. became able to recognize intrusive influences from literature, theatre and music and to relinquish these in favour of artistic means intrinsic to film itself. The early years of German film were marked by sets reminiscent of the theatre with its invisible fourth wall. The constructed Soviet set-pieces by figures such as Eisenstein, Pudovkin etc. did not allow an intrinsically filmic rhythm to develop, as Tarkovsky's accurate critique made clear.[45] Eisenstein's insert material (as in *Ivan the Terrible*) did not use 'sealed chronology' (a key term coined by Tarkovsky), but instead the fantastical presentation of a Wagnerian myth of apocalypse. This is not to say that no film-alien forms of expression are discernible in modern cinema. On the contrary, the quest for genuine filmic expression is rarely of concern or interest to film critics.

3. The imaginative textures emerging in a future art of film, sustained by laws of reincarnation and destiny, cannot offer

the visual spectacle that many expect from cinema. In the same way, Steiner's 'Mystery Plays' appeared to be entirely uninfluenced by the contemporary style of naturalistic theatre as it figured in plays by Ibsen or Hauptmann. Thus the spectator of these Mystery Plays learns practically nothing about the details, otherwise thought so important, of the 'real' private and social life of the chief protagonists.

4. The basic phenomenon of cinematographic recording, which aims to preserve a living movement sequence, along with the associated mirroring problem,[46] remains unaffected by questions of art or commerce. The technical recording of image and tone can equally serve the 'hypnotic monster' (Pasolini)[47] *and* a future art of film. It can testify to supersensible perception in the thoughts and feelings of its protagonists or equally serve to overwhelm the consumer in an inartistic and rigidified realm of the mind. The spirit experienced within the soul can, as the wonderful scene in *American Beauty* by Sam Mendes (1999) shows, also be conjured by an empty plastic bag dancing in front of a dark-red brick wall, which the young character, Ricky, films with his amateur video camera and which, as he says, reveals the 'life in everything and its almost unbearable beauty'.

5. The renewal of film as art form by 'furthering the spiritual in film',[48] can be deduced from the testamentary letter that Steiner wrote to his pupils a few days before he died. (See also the reference to this in Appendix 1.) It was published on 12 April 1925, two weeks after his death, in the news-sheet of the Anthroposophical Society. There we read:

> Our age needs knowledge that goes beyond nature since it must cope inwardly with the dangerous effects of a life that has sunk below the level of nature. Naturally we are not speaking here of returning to former cultural epochs, but of finding ways whereby human beings can create the right relationship both with their cultural conditions and the cosmos. Nowadays very few people indeed feel the important spiritual tasks that are emerging for humankind. Electricity which, after its discovery, was praised as the

> very soul of natural existence, must be recognized as a force
> that can lead from nature down into sub-nature. But as
> human beings we must not slide down with it...

Thus an enlivening of the powers of thinking of future filmmakers by reflecting upon destinies that unfold in a sequence
of lives on earth, as a template for cinematic film compositions
and settings, surely also belongs to the 'important spiritual tasks'
that Steiner refers to.

9

Rudolf Steiner offered strong reasons for his warnings against the tendency to expend one's emotions on 'copies' (associatively adopted thoughts). He offered methods and meditative schooling to illumine subconscious drives and emotional energies, so as to perceive underlying reality-creating elements. If we neglect the task of feeling responsibility for the emergence and effects of our thought contents, this will lead sooner or later to far-reaching consequences.

In grave images, which his listeners at the time can scarcely have seen in specific relation to their inner life, Rudolf Steiner pointed in one of his lectures to a 'spider entity' that would gradually encircle and interweave the globe, and would absorb our sense-bound thinking into the structure of its 'terrible intelligence'.[49] A whole century ago, he said this:

> From the earth will spring a terrible race of entities whose cha-racter will be halfway between the mineral and the plant kingdoms, robotic-type beings with a superfluity of reason, an intense power of reason. They will encircle and conquer the earth like a network and tissue of terrible spiders, but possessing huge wisdom; yet their organization will not even reach as high as plant existence. They will be entangled in each other, and in their outward movements will imitate everything that people have conceived with their shadowy intellect, everything devoid of what should come from a new power of imagination, from spiritual science altogether. All such unreal thoughts that people think will come alive. As the earth is now wrapped in an atmospheric layer of air, so it will then be covered — as is sometimes the case with swarms of locusts — with terrible mineral-plant-type spiders. These will have great perspicacity but will interweave with each other in a very malevolent way. And if people have not enlivened their shadowy intellectual concepts, they will necessarily unite their lives not with the beings who have sought to descend since

the last third of the nineteenth century but with these terrible mineral-plant spider creatures. Human beings themselves will be compelled to co-exist with these spider creatures, and they will have to seek their further progress in world existence in the form of evolution that this spider entity assumes...

Now there are people who see in this description the model for the science-fiction film, *Matrix* (1994) which is admired by many students of anthroposophy. Its creators, the Wachowski sisters, both trans-gender, located their phantasmagorias of physical slime and scorpion implants in illusionary interwoven and parallel worlds. While The Truth is assigned to the original world, and the Matrix to illusionary decline and degeneration in which people are compelled to vegetate, the chief protagonists drive on the story interactively between the worlds without distinction (so that, for instance, it does not matter on which side of the divide between Truth and Matrix one kills a person, since this extinguishes him in both simultaneously).

Similarly, fantastical magical powers can be performed on both sides of the threshold of reality between The Truth and the Matrix, though what most astonished me was how gripped and enthralled the cinema audience was by long-winded battles between the super heroes, accompanied by computer-generated, time-lapse levitation gimmicks.

The Wachowski sisters set their film in the year 2199, whereas Rudolf Steiner, in his non-fantasy commentary, was referring to the eighth millennium AD when, according to his account, the last women capable of giving birth would be born on earth. In its crude esotericism, *Matrix* offers no picture or idea that could help us understand humanity's evolution. Nor do its heroes (Neo, Morpheus and Trinity) give us any comprehensible glimpse into the nature of a spiritually-founded conduct that would qualify them as saviours of humanity. They remain comic caricatures (the film's originators based them on Japanese mangas), with Morpheus understanding everything, Neo nothing, and Trinity believing both. They battle and destroy on behalf of the good, the only sure fact in an otherwise greatly baffling saga.

Hollywood, the financial stronghold for the most expensive western film productions, plays an important role through its accumulated know-how with influential story formats and its strategic dominance in discovering and marketing trend-setting material. In recent years, with the increasing influence of the Far East (the majority of the big studios now belong to Japanese and Chinese investors), its inherited cinema products have been combined with the new digital range that internet-based producers now offer in the field of TV series and video games. Thus what could only previously be seen in the cinema, can be marketed for home consumption on (now already superseded) DVDs or by the 'forward-looking' method of online download.

Major Indian film production from Bollywood primarily focuses on satisfying Asian audiences' need for pictures and narrative, which is substantially different from the demands of western film audiences. It must meet expectations of much longer and more complex narrative forms (with flashbacks and background narratives) interwoven with emotional highs. The usual theme is the bliss of love, and the pain of parting, accompanied by folkloric Indian dance set-pieces and Oriental pop music. The prototype of many western film heroes, a canny careerist or rebel, world-weary and tormented by inner emptiness, an urban loner, is largely absent from Indian cinema. Even if Indian film heroes are plagued by loss, pain and death, they usually work their way towards a reflective happy ending arrived at by karmically appropriate ways. The western film audience regards this as childish kitsch, in contrast to the (equally kitsch) super-cool, western loner with his psychological baggage.

Cinematic visions of the future, which appeal to the largest crowds, lodge themselves deep in their audiences' dreaming thought-life. And since these films cannot stimulate thoughtful appraisal without losing their mass appeal, any testing of their 'truth', or, rather, of the subconscious background to a particular fantasy scenario, is lacking, or avoided on principle.

Learning to distinguish between genuine imaginations and fantastical miasmas is not something that can happen at the cinema itself, but can only be applied there; or most likely not applied. A hindrance to this kind of perceptiveness is an unconscious, unexamined acquiescence in the portrayal of a future where man and machine will be ever more 'bio-electrically' entwined, something inspired by a grim transhumanism that figures in dozens of powerful science-fiction films of recent years. This scenario simply 'deposits' itself in the psyche and thought-life of audiences, and, residing there unless it is understood and corrected, acts with unconscious manipulation so that the viewer is already unquestioningly accepting and succumbing to many seemingly inevitable future phenomena affecting both individuals and society as a whole.

I want to highlight a few examples of how big film productions co-opt the thinking of their audiences by means of a precise, visualized anticipation of future human conditions. Solely by the fact that these scenarios are located in some undefined future enables them to meet a problematic thirst for distraction and entertainment.

With Ridley Scott's *Blade Runner* (1992), Hollywood initiated the financially very lucrative cyberpunk genre. Blade Runner is set in Los Angeles in 2019 (around the turn of the millennium, it seemed to be time to bring everything rapidly forward). Genetically engineered human beings, called replicants, with no immigration rights to earth citizenship, are making problems. These replicants are far superior to human beings, both physically and mentally, and have therefore been furnished, as a precaution, with only a shortened lifespan of four years. They are primarily employed to conquer other planets and realms for humanity. But now they seem to have formed a liking for the earth, which is a cause of much annoyance.

The financial and legal background to *Blade Runner* is very complex, which is why the official Director's Cut — whose ending differs markedly from the official cinema release — did not appear until 2000. The cinema film ends with a replicant hunter eliminating the last replicant after the latter, in a 'very human' way, has granted him life before his own fast approaching death arrives. Then the hero, who is likely to face state sanctions for his own independent actions, successfully makes his escape. The end of Ridley Scott's Director's Cut, on the other hand, leaves us uncertain as to whether he manages to escape, and this is compounded by the possibility that the escaping protagonist might also himself be a replicant.

In Amenàbar's *Obre los Ojos* ('Open Your Eyes', 1997, remake by Cameron Crowe as *Vanilla Sky*, 2001), the film ends in 2145 with the chief protagonist, a suicide who has 'in reality' been cryonically stored in deep refrigeration to await rebirth, once again hurling himself from the top of a skyscraper in order to escape a misguided programme that has given him life in a virtual world. The screenplay author declined to reveal what happens after the 'death' of a virtual consciousness that has lived outside of its corpse for a hundred and fifty years. The film ends, after the body hits the ground, with a black screen and the prompting to 'Obre los Ojos!'

Spielberg's *Minority Report* (2002) takes place in 2054. Crimes are no longer committed since the mere intention for them is perceived by three clairvoyant women who have hallucinatory visions as they swim plant-like in a special fluid. The prophetic nightmares of these 'Precogs' as they are called, provide information about thought criminals who are then arrested by the police before they can commit murder, and are then kept in an enduring intermediate state… until of course something goes wrong.[50]

In *Transcendence* (2014), fuzzy terms are used to explain how transcendence, as 'technological singularity', can assure the advance of materialistic biocomputer research. This is prevented by attacks from a 'reactionary, anti-science' party. The leading transhumanist (played by Johnny Depp) who is tinkering with the creation of living, computer-steered robots, is killed. Following this, efforts focus on the challenging enterprise of uploading his 'undead' brain onto the laboratory computer.

These and similar films, with their fantastical narratives, smooth the way for acceptance of future 'transhuman' projects, which seek by new means to realize the old Fascist dream of creating a race of superhumans or at least of people with the 'required' qualities.

By contrast, recent decades have seen a few film directors whose sense of responsibility led them to take a different path. In their films they started to portray their feeling perceptions in artistic form, governed by efforts to develop awareness of individual consciousness — a key undertaking today. Among them were some, too, who sought in their portrayals of the future to correct the crazy fantasies of the transhumanists.[51] One can perhaps imagine some pleasing results if Steiner were to meet such filmmakers and could stimulate them to make films that realize 'the laws of destiny in the course of recurring incarnations' in an artistic cinematic sequence of scenes.

An art of film based on true imaginative insights could in future help to make people aware of the palpable deficiencies of transhumanism,[52] and the temptations attendant on it. The dogmatic ideology underlying transhumanism in the form of a denial of pure, active thinking and human self-determination, makes the missionary zeal of its proponents to use the development of artificial intelligence for human progress seem like a crusade against our capacity for independent cognition and self-reflection. So far none of this movement's representatives have been willing or able to make a clear distinction between human thinking based on a subliminal I-creating activity and inwardly observing intuition, and the electronically controlled operations of a programmed robot. Since, in their dogmatic stance, they refuse to study the processes by which their thoughts, feelings and action motivations arise, they also fail to understand why a robot will never be able to have intuitions. They understand only how a computer functions, and that it can solve quicker than a person problems that, like chess, involve computational accomplishments based on a fixed conceptual starting point. And even if they concede that a robot will never need a moral education, they are unable to offer any comprehensible, experientially based explanation for this.

A worldview that subconsciously appropriates the idea of the spirit-devoid action of intelligence will invariably seek to suppress human self-determination. Transhumanism necessarily erases the boundary between man and machine by placing such little value on this distinction.

The 'moral' demands of transhumanism, as we find them everywhere in science-fiction screenplay scripts since *E.T.* (1982) — such as 'Love the aliens even in their subhuman ugliness' — are based largely on technology-loving sentimentality and are to a large degree consciousness-dulling. Missionary zeal is also responsible for the dream future expressed in the following words of a dubious champion of transhumanism:

> I see these machines as our successors. At present people scarcely believe this since the machines are only as intelligent as insects. But as time passes we will discover the great potential that they contain. And we will like our new robots since they will be more pleasant than people. There is after all no need to build in to these machines all the negative human attributes that have existed since the stone age ... A robot will be a much more social being than many people. So you see, we will like them, and will identify with them. We will accept them as our children, albeit ones who have not been formed by our genes but whom we have built with our hands and mind.[53]

Given the fact that investment capital in the film industry is always on the look-out for new themes and theses, it seems astonishing that its screenplay departments have taken a rather 'unprofessional' stance toward modes of spiritual narration that contrast with transhumanist fantasy. In other words, despite potential interest from audiences, they have appeared lost for ideas here. Transhumanism conveys the picture of a blissful humanity under the yoke of authoritarian suppression, vegetating aimlessly in company with biomechanoids reared by technocrats, the 'mixed race' of the future. Such a prospect is scarcely welcomed by anyone so far.

In a survey by a big weekly magazine in Germany two decades ago already, more than 60 percent of those questioned by no means rejected the idea of reincarnation as nonsense but said it was perfectly imaginable. Thus this ideologically driven self-censorship by Hollywood explains why its trend scouts have not long ago proposed films that would lend human evolution a countenance capable of healing the hallucinations of a transhumanist future. Curious and eager screenplay authors could have learned much from the laws of reincarnation and karma that Rudolf Steiner investigated. One outcome of this might have been, at least, the recognition that humanity cannot evolve further either through genetic breeding or through computer-assisted implants but solely by deepening spiritual self-knowledge and seeking individual freedom; for which, given the spiritually impoverished condition of our contemporaries — amongst whom we count ourselves — many successive lives will no doubt be needed.

When creating his *Star Wars Saga*, George Lucas was one of the few to draw on his reading of Rudolf Steiner's works (we will come back to Tarkovsky later). *Star Wars* has been the most lucrative and successful series in the whole history of cinema. Privately, Lucas has given active support to the Waldorf teacher training seminar in Sacramento, California, and sent his children to a Waldorf school. The creative group that first developed the *Star Wars* mythology, instigated by his wife at the time, Marcia Lucas, involved people who were familiar with Steiner's work. The following comes from the transcript of an initial meeting they held:

1. Marcia is familiar with anthroposophy and the work of Rudolf Steiner, and needs our help to create the screenplay [...].
2. She added: 'The cinema should be used to convey important messages to the public, and to relate a spiritual narrative that has good foundations in reality.'[54]

Star Wars presents its cosmic drama as a profane technical fantasy, and although Lucas gained much from Rudolf Steiner's spiritual science, he avoided referring to it in any detail, no doubt because of anxiety that this might be bad for business.

The duality of evil, which in Steiner's *Occult Science* is presented as a battle waged for possession of the human being in the world of spirit between Ahriman and Lucifer, appears in *Star Wars* as the opposition between 'Jabba' and 'Vader', whose characteristics strongly resemble those described by Steiner.

10

We have mentioned films that show inner affinities with the spiritual-scientific research of Steiner without however posing the decisive question as to whether merely incorporating the theme of reincarnation and karma in cinematic portrayal already gives rise to work of high artistic quality. Or, to put it differently, can films located amidst, say, public transport, the lives of small traders, and solicitors' offices, or in urban ghettos with a cast of prostitutes and petty crooks, or films that conjure heroic deeds of ancient times, or simply stage a comedy of love, all equally be examples of great film art?

Are there authentic means of expression intrinsic to the art of film? And if these exist, can we discern them through the narrative style employed or the images conveyed? Few film directors have said much about this. They have all learned from the films they have seen, and have added their own contribution to what remains, fundamentally, an enigmatic pictorial form of narrative. And those among them whose films indisputably testify to the quest for a true art of film — Pasolini, Bresson, Tarkovsky, Godard, Kurosawa, Allen, Cassavetes, Wenders, Malick and many others — have given expression both in their film work and in their comments about it, to things that are often very contradictory.

Pasolini, more sensitive than anyone to the anti-artistic potential of visual fodder, and always looking for the syntax of a 'poetic film', seemed in some of his last films to be trying to subvert himself. Shortly before he was murdered, he distanced himself from them. The great ascetic of film art, Robert Bresson, whom Tarkovsky revered above all others, condemned film-set artificialities — including the use of professional actors — as artistic barbarism, but admitted in a passing remark that the James Bond film, *For Your Eyes Only* had given him great pleasure. Tarkovsky, to whom we owe several far-reaching analyses of time perception as an otherwise scarcely considered foundation of cinematic art, ends his work with a film shot in Sweden that possesses little cinematic originality and is overfreighted with moral symbols. It is as if *The Sacrifice* were a Bergman film from the 60s resurrected in colour.

While Ingmar Bergman, Federico Fellini, Michelangelo Antonioni, Theo Angelopoulos, Alfred Hitchcock, John Huston, Éric Rohmer, David Lynch and Stanley Kubrick — to name a few others — made many interesting comments on the details of filmmaking, they avoided general statements about the nature, task and potential of cinema. In some of their films — cited by many of their followers as evidence of a developing art of film — we encounter them as artists on a quest for spiritual knowledge. One of the substantial differences here between their work and the consumer products of the visual entertainment industry is no doubt that the latter must avoid any personal concern intruding into their films.

In one of her last pieces of writing, American cultural critic Susan Sontag expressed the following thesis, that the distinctive lunacy, the almost religious worship of cinema, French cinephilia of the 1960s, is what gave rise for a while to European films that stirred people into a state of indubitable emotional sublimity. This genre of 'Art House' cinema, which briefly engendered a great flowering of cinematic artistry and creativity, vanished again the moment cinema was no longer revered as a place of self-discovery and love. The term 'Art House' cinema still survives, but only 'cultural intercourse' of such a kind could really bring it back to life again.[55]

There would be several things to say about this 'cultural act of love'. And in doing so we could not overlook the Art House films of the 60s, so much part of their time and so justifiably fascinating. They cannot be separated from the generally inspiring power that took hold at the time of literature, pop music and theatre. This had its source in inspirational occurrences in the supersensible world, which moved artists to more or less conscious representation and embodiment of artistic and cultural convulsion — to which they themselves looked back with astonishment for several decades.

It is understandable and no cause for regret if a younger generation now no longer relates to the individualistic cultural thrust of the past century but instead embraces Tarantino's genre spectacles, Jackson's films of Tolkien's works, and new, ambitious film formats of TV-series length which were first established by Lynch's *Twin Peaks* (1990) — such as *Gilmore Girls* (The WB), *The Wire* (HBO), *Breaking Bad* (AMC), *Sense8* (Netflix) etc.

If we look to films for indications of a general human striving we can find these in the stories of film directors who like making pronouncements. That is, for instance, in Rohmer's idea of individual destiny, which governs the mercurial relationships of his deluded lovers; in Godard's quaintly melancholic intellectualism, which overlays French urbane banality with a brash, stylized imagistic and cultural shorthand; in the decadent yet stylistically assured melancholia of the question pervading Antonioni's films of a slumbering spiritual existence underlying dull civic society; in Lynch's obsessions with the fantastical interplay of different mental states in which a contact with objective reality is lost or was never sought in the first place; in the panopticon of amiably eccentric vanities that emerge through Fellini's dream-mist; or in Bergman's existentialist quest for God, obscured by divisions between the sexes etc., etc., etc.

But the instinctiveness that largely characterizes the emergence of these filmmaker profiles at the same time reduces their depth and thus their capacity to convincingly represent the kinds of problems decisively affecting our era. The same can be discerned in the psychology of their central film characters. How easily audiences are gripped by protagonists' pathological traits, and how rarely do we meet in film heroes any compellingly portrayed — that is, experientially valid — overcoming of egoistic limitations, in which, anyway, ordinary consciousness finds little interest.

Pathological dispositions are even discussed in detail in relation to some of the most important film directors, and sometimes even by themselves. This is true, for instance, of Alfred Hitchcock, Walt Disney, Roman Polanski, Woody Allen, Lars von Trier, Quentin Tarantino etc. This is not to support the platitude that a great artist must always be somewhat crazy. Tarkovsky, by contrast — typically Russian in this — never tired of referring to the moral and spiritual influence of true works of art:

> Whether or not a director possesses depth becomes apparent in his reasons for shooting films. How he does this and the method he employs is entirely beside the point... Unspiritual art already contains its own tragedy. The very recognition of our era's lack of spirituality demands a certain spirituality of the artist. The real artist always serves immortality: he tries to render this world and the people living in it immortal. But if by contrast he does not embark on the search for absolute truth, instead exchanging global aims for trivialities, he will remain nothing but a one-day wonder.

Tarkovsky's profound sense of Christian morality came to expression neither in the Orthodox Church nor any other confession, nor was he driven by a theologically ossified 'quest for God' (unlike the Catholic influence on early Bresson or the underlying Protestantism of Bergman). In Tarkovsky's view, an initiatory religiosity is inseparably connected with the social task of the artist:

> A truly artistic idea is always something that torments the artist, indeed, can be almost life-threatening. Its realization can be compared only with a decisive and momentous step in life. It has always been so, for all who engaged with art.

And in relation to the film artist's *criminal responsibility*, of which Tarkovsky spoke, he wrote:

> The art of film is still seeking its own expression, only occasionally getting anywhere near it. To this day the question of a specific language of film remains open. And this book, too, only offers a further attempt at clarification in this field. At all events, the state of modern cinema repeatedly prompts us to reconsider the value of the art of cinema.

Tarkovsky's quest for truth in art came to compelling expression in *Andrei Rublev*, *The Mirror* and *Stalker* — not in a triumphant register but in something more melancholic and reverent. Thus,

Andrei Tarkovsky and Robert Bresson, two great, moralists of the cinema, in Cannes 1983.

for instance, the three protagonists in *Stalker* enter the mysterious, enigmatic 'zone' in which the soul begins to breathe, though not its inmost realm where all wishes are fulfilled. The tragic element here lies not in the failure to satisfy their egoistic desires but rather in the simultaneous expression of their lack of knowledge of their true, inmost desires, culminating in the love of inner freedom. It may be that my interpretation here is at odds with Tarkovsky's own; with a trace of resignation he stated that the 'zone' which transforms the film shot up to that point in black and white into sudden colour, is not a symbol but simply life itself which we either endure or are destroyed by. The capacity to distinguish essential from inessential things — by which is meant spiritually essential or sensory and transient things — leads, says Tarkovsky, to us coping and enduring life (the 'zone'):

> Nothing is symbolized in any of my films. The 'zone' in *Stalker* is simply the 'zone'. It is life, through which we have to pass,

in which we either go under or endure. And whether or not we persevere and endure depends on our sense of self-worth, our ability to distinguish the essential from the incidental.[56]

If we wanted to equate symbols with daily sensory existence, the 'zone' may indeed be life itself. But it would then still remain incomprehensible why the three chosen ones take such great risk on themselves in order to enter the 'inner realm' of the 'zone'. Nor is there any need for a compelling wish for the life 'through which we have to pass' since, with every breath they take, they demonstrate how much they are attached to life.

My medium-length film, LYDIA, created in the summer of 1968, has a comparable initiatory key. Here too there is a 'zone', a tunnel through which the chief protagonist must find his way. The ordinary sensory mind has no access to the zone, which is a transition to an exceptional spiritual condition and to experience of higher knowledge that emerges thereafter.[57] Only at the second attempt does the chief protagonist, with blindfold eyes, find the entrance to the tunnel behind the cemetery, passing through it attentively and, on emerging from it, finding himself in a magically rejuvenated world. The following words accompany his dance in front of, and with, a soldier's memorial carved in stone: 'Let us not be carried away. Cleansing and salving flashes of illumination, and slaughtering embraces that melt all contradictions are rare, for the way is hard into the city of Soho, the city that matters.' By 'the way' is meant the gradual spiritualization of the sense world, undertaken in freedom. That the life span of a single incarnation is not sufficient to achieve this becomes apparent to all who consider what it involves. An initial, seemingly brilliant soaring into a world of higher dimensions can be no more than the first step in undertaking our real task: that of becoming a fully conscious citizen of two worlds.

Here the question arises about the cinematic 'material' to which artistic shape must be given. Tarkovsky, who starts from a classical definition of art — 'An artwork signifies in every instance the organic interplay of idea and form'[58] — said the following:

...A painter knows that the colours are his material, and a writer, likewise, is very much aware that the weapon of his effect upon the public is the word. Only we filmmakers are not yet absolutely certain about the 'material' from which a future film will be 'formed'.[59]

In saying this he echoes all previous film theorists who have given the matter serious consideration.

Christian Metz ends his fundamental work *Language and Cinema* inconclusively: 'Is the cinema a language or not? That is an issue of dispute now superseded. But it is one that should be expanded and at the same time examined in more precise detail.' And: 'Whether cinema involves reproduction or creation, it will always stand either before or beyond language.'[60]

As we will come to see more clearly, solution of the problem of aesthetics specific to film is connected with Rudolf Steiner's cinema-related intuition and intention. Here it should first be pointed out that the chasm between 'reproduction' and 'creation', between an Impressionist or Expressionist approach to the art of cinema, is apparent already in the very earliest films.[61] One-sided fixation on one of the two tendencies prevents the emergence of a free art of cinema. Tarkovsky puts it like this: 'Artists can be grouped into those who shape their own world, and those who *reproduce* reality. I myself without doubt belong to the first.'[62] I beg to differ since Tarkovsky, in my view, is an artist able to establish a balance between reproduction and creation in every one of his films. Elsewhere he himself expressed this, albeit in a veiled way: 'In cinema, the image is based on an ability to present one's own *feeling* of an object as *observation*.'[63]

Robert Bresson said the following at the press conference in Cannes in 1974: 'Now that we have the great inventions of camera and magnetophone, our material must be sought elsewhere than in "photographic images of actors who perform some illusory comedy before us".' In his films, Bresson was seeking what he called a 'cinematographic script', the script of life. The Danes still speak of the cinema today as 'biography', abbreviated to 'bio', which in Greek signifies the 'script of life' Bresson was looking for. According to him, this cannot emerge if the filmmaker seeks only to 'photographically' record ideas he already possessed before the moment of shooting. Cinema made in this way is for Bresson not art and not cinematography, but merely cinema. Thus Bresson employs a really very private nomenclature to make a distinction that appears to him to be very important.

If, for instance, we watch his film *Lancelot du Lac*, which met with both acclaim and disdain at Cannes in 1974 (the selection committee initially refused to accept it), this distinction from 'mere cinema' becomes immediately apparent. There is nothing of the cinematic medieval era as we expect it, and we become aware how greatly films inform the way we envisage past historical periods: how, say, a knight enters a hall, how he must bow before the Lord and Lady, how he mounts a horse, how he brings it to a halt, how people eat and laugh at long wooden trestles, how they fight battles or have secret assignations between stone pillars. Nothing of this in Bresson's film: the shots present observations made in the moment's immediacy — for instance the sensory details that interested Bresson as horses turned, the hooves or hind parts of the horse, and then, say, the clash of a suit of armour, anxiety and uncertainty as an unknown knight appears on the horizon, the unstylized groaning and moaning during jousts.

Bresson always took measures to plan nothing in advance before he appeared on the set. Sometimes he did not even decide beforehand what scenes were to be filmed. And so there were often waiting periods for the team until Bresson found a new orientation that took him by surprise. He trusted that the sense of fresh perception and lack of stress would communicate itself to cinema-goers. He never called his films 'works' always only 'studies' — attempts at something whose direction was more or less clear to him. From early on he kept actors away from his camera. He found that they attached themselves in too unnatural a way to their ideas of their roles, which he said he did not examine in advance because they only came to life during the cinematographic work. He said actors would always 'perform' without really knowing what was involved. For similar reasons Pasolini also largely shot films with lay people;

and David Lynch hides from his actors their roles and functions in the overall context. He urges them to enter into life situations whose underlying reasons and connections remain unknown to them.

The first time I saw Bresson's *Lancelot du Lac*, what surprised me was how a far more intense sense of medieval times emerged from it than would have done from a highly accurate historical reconstruction. Tarkovsky's film about an icon painter, *Andrei Rublev*, conjures a past era with similar persuasiveness, as does Pasolini in his fantastical re-imaginings of archaic Greek periods (*Odysseus Rex, Medea*) or of the time around the birth of Christ in Jerusalem, in his film *The Gospel According to St. Matthew.*

The controversy between cinema's documentary versus scene-staging potency arose the moment it was born. Though different directors show strong preferences for one or the other, the question about the art of film inevitably remains separate from such preferences. There are, after all, examples in which both styles or approaches are used together, or are interwoven.

One of the two roots of cinematic expression emerged for the first time in autonomous form in the work of Georges Méliès, to whom Martin Scorsese dedicated his film *Hugo*. Méliès, successful to begin with as a conjuror and illusionist at fairs, was the inventor of many cinematic tricks such as time lapse, stop-motion, coloured film emulsions, dual lighting and cross-fading etc, which, drawing on the novels of Jules Verne, he used in his Paris studio for his fantasy films (*Trip to the Moon, Impossible Voyage*). This approach, entirely based on staging and set creation, was developed further in France particularly, as an extension of its great theatrical tradition. (For instance, Éric Rohmer wrote and staged numerous stage plays as did Ingmar Bergman and other film directors.)

The essays by André Bazin (1918–1958) also concern the importance of staging based on the influence of painting. He was an influential film theorist of the Nouvelle Vague, and the founder and chief editor of the *Cahiers du cinema* (from 1951 onward). His reflections on 'horizontal montage' through mise-en-scène (e.g. in a tracking shot), as an extension and expansion of 'Russian' vertical montage (Eisenstein, Pudovkin) influenced numerous film directors such as Godard, Rohmer, Bresson and Tarkovsky.

The second root of film introduces the power of documentary to cinema,[64] and was something to which the Lumière brothers paid homage.[65] It established its own film sector, that of the documentary film in a narrower sense. In so-called 'fake documentaries' (such as *Blair Witch Project*, 1999) its stylistic characteristics are also employed for fictions, which are therefore no longer perceived as 'true fictions'

Georges Méliès (1861—1938)

and can lead to considerable annoyance on the part of viewers. The *Bourne* films (2002 to 2016) were the first to convincingly employ a documentary camera style 'close' to unfolding events, so as to elicit from the viewer a sense that what is being depicted is more 'credible'. This aimed to make audiences temporarily forget that they were watching a feature film. They should, rather, feel themselves to be a concealed visual partner with the cameraman who is operating in a dangerous situation.

Manipulative deceptions such as those mentioned are rejected by film directors who see films as 'certified' verities

The Lumière brothers, Auguste and Jean (1962, 1864–1948, 1954)

inscribed by life itself, which give the viewer privileged insight into a reality undistorted by staging and illusion. Reproduction, 'mere photography' as Bresson called it, is for many film directors the chief adversary of their art. Those who see the practice of art in creation and not in repetition of something already existing, will find this self-evident. But we have to delve deeper into 'cinematic creation' since without the reproduction of sensory reality which constitutes a film, no cinema would exist at all (unless we include a few examples from the 60s of the last century when 'filmmakers' worked directly with the chemical emulsion of the film base). Likewise the commercially so successful hyperrealism of animation films, or CGI-supported animation, rely fully on photographic and graphic models.

Following this look at some of the general conditions of a hypothetical art of film, I will now turn to particular statements by film directors that seem to confirm Rudolf Steiner's reflections on cinema's capacities and potential. Let me reiterate that this lies in the manifestation of the laws of destiny and reincarnation.

Vogelsang's showcase

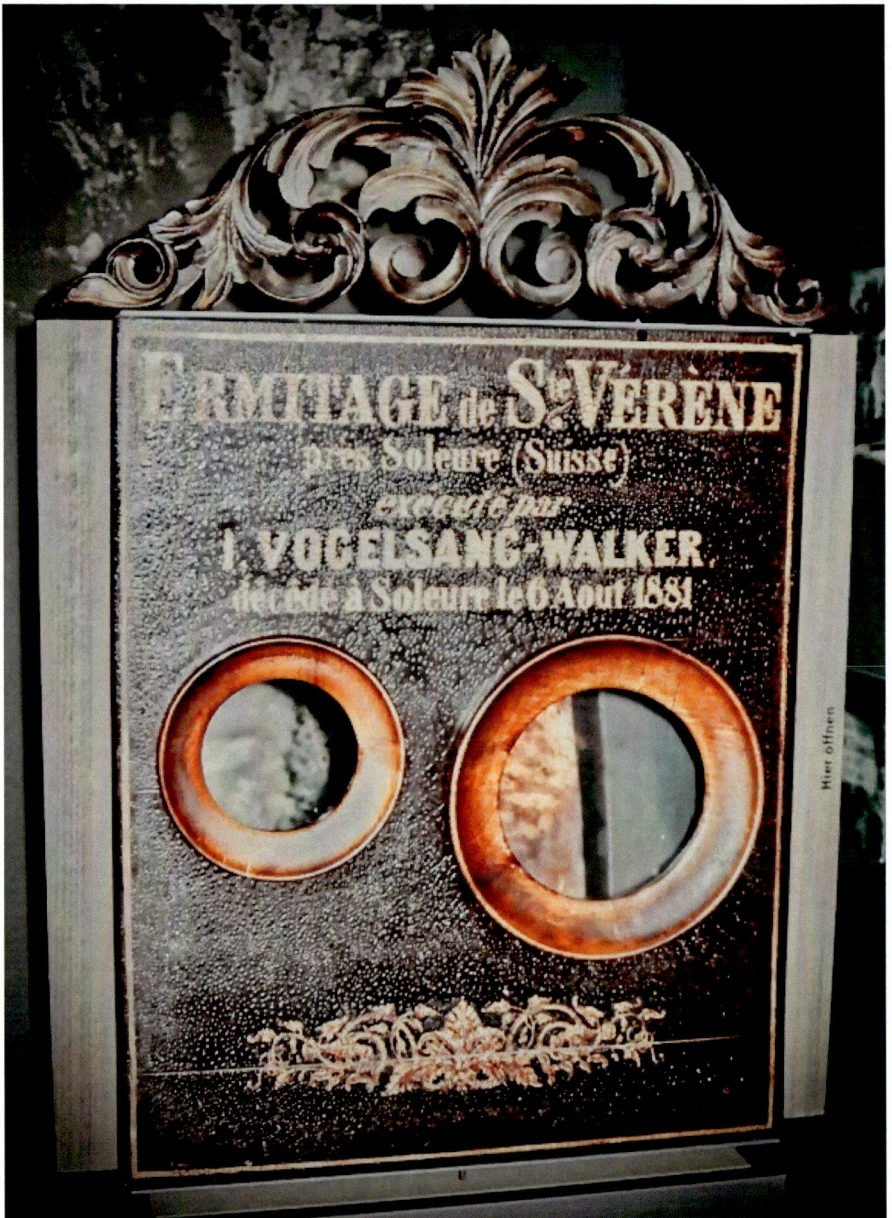

Insight into Vogelsang's showcase: the Hermitage St. Verène

In the Hermitage St. Verène: a scene from the film Stella da Falla (1971).
The author is on the left and Brother Niklaus on the right

Scene from Stella da Falla. The arrival in modern times is sealed with the purchase of a film camera

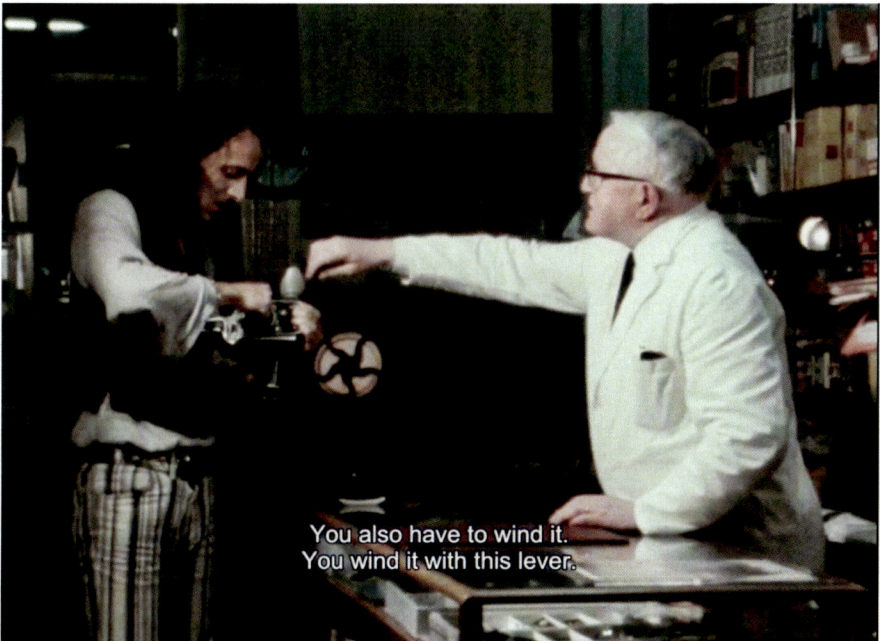

Jan Stuten, from his image cycle Furcht

11

We have heard how sensitive the Italian filmmaker Pier Paolo Pasolini was to the disruptive influence of film, and film's modern relatives, on free artistic expression.[66] In connection with this he spoke profoundly about the question of a possible 'language of film'. He did so repeatedly in correspondence with his 'spiritual brother', the semiologist and successful novelist Umberto Eco. With the following words, Pasolini rejected the latter's

Pier Paolo Pasolini (1922–1975)

'nominalism of universals',[67] transposed back into the medieval era in his novel, *The Name of the Rose*:

> ...Here I must also say what I think about death (and the reader is free to ask, sceptically, what this has to do with film). I have said on various occasions, and always unfortunately expressed myself badly, that reality has its own language; that this in fact is a language that requires a 'general semiology' to grasp it, the term for which is so far lacking. (*And here taking issue with Eco, he notes*:) The semiologists always distinguish distinct and precisely delineated objects in the same way as diverse, already existing symbolic languages. They have not yet discovered that semiology could be a descriptive science of reality.[68]
>
> In poor formulations always, I have said that this language, in so far as it relates to the human being, coincides with our

actions. This means that we express ourselves through our actions not in a pragmatic sense but because we modify reality thereby, and this works back upon our mind and spirit. But this action of ours lacks unity or also coherence until it has been completed… In other words, as long as we have a future, that is, an unknown dimension, we remain unexpressed…Thus it is absolutely necessary to die because, as long as we live, we lack meaning, and the language of our life (through which we express ourselves and to which we accord the greatest significance) remains incomprehensible: a chaos of possibilities, a quest for relationships and signifiers without the solution of continuity. Death creates a fulminant montage of our life; that is, it selects its truly signifying moments (and now no longer through other moments that are contradictory, incoherent or can be relativized) and places them in a sequence and context. Only thanks to death does our life serve to express us.[69]

Pasolini speaks of a spiritually active lawfulness that shines on the life that has been lived, the light of a post-death capacity of discernment, distinguishing between essential and inessential, progressive and retrogressive, so as to achieve (by implication for a subsequent life) a projected *solution through continuity*.[70] He emphasizes the enactment of a compelling karmic lawfulness, and sees in death the prerequisite for becoming aware of this. He tries to persuade his interviewer that this karmic lawfulness exists by comparing it with the art of film, and the picture sequences only finally evaluated by their montage, corresponding to life experiences. Pasolini's tragedy was to have perceived what modern people lack — a fully conscious, scientific enlarge-ment of our powers of cognition, which would enable us to assimilate the 'laws of destiny and reincarnation'.[71] This is clear from the way in which he saw his whole sense of himself as connected with destiny and reincarnation. In the excerpt from an interview below, the tragedy that moves and motivates him becomes audible.

Pier Paolo Pasolini was not fortunate enough to encounter in his lifetime in their modern, re-founded form the sacred values that were current in the ancient world, that glimmered again briefly in the ecstasies of Franciscanism's ascetic renunciation, and were at last liberated in a spiritual science that dispelled the 'dogmas of the old humanism'.

> *Pasolini:* When I insist so greatly on my homesickness for the sacred, this is because I remain faithful to the old values. Sometimes I have the feeling that these have been sacrificed to an artificially accelerated evolution, to a wrongly premature forgetfulness.
>
> *Interviewer:* Your attachment to past forms does not exclude a use of references to linguistics and science. I am thinking here also of your deep interest in semiology.
>
> *P:* Semiology, let us mention in passing, is still founded on the old values. It is nothing more nor less than a science in the same way as all other disciplines of our old humanism, into which I was born and with which I grew up.
>
> *I:* What do you think is preventing the emergence of these new values?
>
> *P:* It is largely our complete inability…to live in the future, and the fact that we can create nothing without reference to our past.
>
> *I:* So the present is the time of ambiguity, of the moment of collapse and disintegration?
>
> *P:* It is hell.

In 1969, Pasolini wrote the screenplay for the first film by his friend Sergio Citti (who often worked on Pasolini's films as a dialogue developer and director's assistant). Pasolini's screenplay ends with one of the two protagonist brothers killing the other with a wooden stick in a passionate fit of jealousy. This happens in the early dawn. The two have been warming themselves at a fire that they lit from twigs and sticks they collected. The film that followed bore the name of the place where this Cain-like act was meant to have happened, *Ostia*. On Sunday morning, 2 November 1975, in open fields near Ostia, not far from the sea, the body of Pier Paolo Pasolini was discovered. The initial court medical report established that death was caused by 'a long, wooden object'.

Eric Rohmer, aged 72, on the set of
Conte d'hiver *(1992)*

The films of the French director Éric Rohmer (1920–2010) testify to a buoyant preoccupation with the question of love and morality, or of morality in love. With a serene, Olympian insight into documentary mise-en-scène, Rohmer takes pleasure in his numerous films in following the astonishing interventions of winged Cupid, and in recounting the wooing, passions and sufferings of his yearning lovers. These are usually young, insecure couples who find each other, and who, without life-threatening collapses or self-destructive dynamics — which often otherwise figure in films on such themes — break up and move on to their next adventures.

In Rohmer's world, male and female students, mathematics teachers and female vintners, single mothers and unremarkable employees, indulge their passionate yearning to maintain their state of infatuation from one moment to the next, and usually fail to do so. And in tune with the French mentality, there is insistent advice from friends, who make active efforts to pair up couples, to attain a happiness in love that all seek but scarcely anyone succeeds in maintaining. The wooing scenes do not shy away from insights into male outlooks that frequently collide with the compelling instincts of women, the latter little concerned with logically-founded rationales and motivations.

The viewer is astonished at the optimism with which these illusionary idealists pursue their hopes of love toward a seemingly boundless future. Their mercurial goings-on, conjured in a permanent mood of spring (whose register has affinities with the recent films of Woody Allen) stand in the greatest possible contrast to the pathological relationships figured in films by Ingmar Bergman, in which couples, long since fallen out of love, endure painful intimacies traceable to mistakes and failings for which both were responsible.

The figures in Rohmer's panopticon only cultivate solitude in brief moments, and survive it with rationalizing confabulations. In doing so they bring all kinds of transient knowledge to bear on their situation. But through all the superficial froth shines the longing they harbour for a stable and lasting love, and for true perception of life and reality. If, rather than identifying with Rohmer's characters, we sense the director's stance as he relates his narratives, we will clearly discern the underlying theme of a superordinate destiny (and in some films, in addition, the reality of reincarnation).

Rohmer, a Catholic like Bresson and like him too a great admirer of Blaise Pascal, called one of his early cycles — a sequence of six films — *Contes moraux* ('Moral Tales'). A later one, consisting for four films was called *Contes des quatre saisons* ('Tales of the Four Seasons'). The latter show Rohmer at the height of his powers and are grand examples of unembellished narrative art. All of them low-budget films, they display Rohmer's ability to captivate the viewer with the flow of his ever-changing occurrences. In the ease with which he documents poorly considered impulses and desires, the quiet sense emerges of a Parnassian, spiritual overview that shows the same distanced affection for all the protagonists.

A further indication of Rohmer's spirituality lies in the way he incorporates nature into his films. In his last cycle Rohmer very much gives the impression that the seasons themselves, that is, the relationship between sun and earth, are collaborators in his love stories. Once he hinted at this, saying that 'nature comes toward human beings', pointing to 'organized nature, which is focused on a goal. The human being is not the master of his matter; his matter is moving in a particular direction.'[72]

Shots of a calm or tumultuous sea, of cloud formations, of a beach puddle or raindrops splashing on asphalt: these are not stylistic interjections as in Godard, not points of entry into a magical world as in Tarkovsky but sure indications that natural phenomena belong to the life of human desires and share an atmospheric unity with the happiness or suffering that proceeds from them.

For Delphine, the young Parisian secretary in *The Green Ray* (1986), failed attempts to spend the summer holidays away from Paris only take a surprising turn when she spontaneously trusts a young man who chats her up at a railway station (she was actually heading back to Paris at the time). By going with him she is able to experience an unusual natural spectacle. At the end of the film she finds peace and fulfilment, as she observes with her new-found friend the rare sight of the 'green ray' upon the sea.

In the first story of *Four Adventures of Reinette and Mirabelle* (1987), the young farmer's wife, Reinette, meets the Parisian Mirabelle who is on holiday in the neighbourhood. They become friends, and Reinette wants to seal her friendship by showing Mirabelle the *heure bleue*, the 'blue hour' which the latter has never heard of. For this they have to get up in the middle of the night, since the *heure bleue* lasts only a few moments before the night sky starts growing bright and the first tentative birds start to twitter. The stillness of this moment is incomparable, says Reinette, and bursts into tears when she fails to show it to Mirabelle since a lorry driving past dispels its natural wonder.

Rohmer's potential understanding of Rudolf Steiner's intention comes to expression most clearly in one of his season films. *Conte d'hiver* (1992), 'A Tale of Winter', starts in the summer holidays in Brittany, where Félicie, a hairdresser, falls in love with an American, Charles. A slip-up when they exchange addresses has serious consequences: Charles cannot find Félicie again. The actual film starts five years after this and shows daily life in Paris around Christmas time. The relationship with Charles led to the birth of Félicie's daughter. Félicie tries to position her life and finances between two men: one is Maxence, her boss, who divorces his wife to open a new hairdressing salon in a provincial city. She agrees to go with him and travels to him in Nevers, only to regret the move bitterly a few days later, and return to Paris to seek support from Loïc, an unmarried Catholic librarian. All in her circle urge her to make a decision. But she doesn't have any sense that a choice or decision is involved here, which, as she says, has already been made. She still exclusively loves her daughter's vanished father. But the way in which she relates to the two men with little consideration, may elicit the viewer's dislike, since there is very little of the image of faithful Penelope in it. Yet Félicie never gives up hope that her Odysseus will return to her. The day after she has been with Loïc to see a moving performance of Shakespeare's *Winter's Tale*, she meets her lost Charles again in a bus, face-to-face as passengers!

It is very inspiring to see how Rohmer subsequently succeeds in conjuring in his actors — that is, Félicie, her daughter, the grandmother, Charles, the relatives who come to the grandmother's flat to celebrate Christmas — such a subtle and convincing sense of emotional occasion triggered by the lightning stroke of destiny. (Here too, it is true to say, as very generally and throughout, that the idea emerging from the whole film contrasts powerfully with what occurs in processes of virtual reality.) Here our indignation about the unappealing conduct that Félicie has previously shown her two other lovers may be dispelled in the light of her well-founded trust that she would meet Charles again.

For the purposes of our account, it is worth mentioning a conversation involving Loïc and a couple of his acquaintance who have invited him and Félicie for supper. The woman brings the conversation round to reincarnation, in which she believes, but is a theme that drives Loïc round the bend. As she tries to persuade him that reincarnation does not contradict Christianity, he refuses to engage any further with the 'claptrap of an Asiatic sect'. His argument is that 'living without responsibility is unchristian, and one can only take responsibility for a single life'. At this point Félicie surprisingly joins the conversation. She usually thinks of herself as being too uneducated to take part in 'academic conversations'. But she disagrees with Loïc's comment and says: 'I'm sure the human spirit needs several lives to really evolve. And we human beings bear responsibility for this evolution.'

Conte d'hiver is one seedling of a genre of film that Rudolf Steiner was seeking to initiate. If such germinal attempts could be developed further, the viewer could experience in various forms how chance occurrences in space and time reveal themselves to be destiny-shaping events. What this signifies for the development of the art of film will be the subject of our further deliberations.

But before we return to Steiner's intentions again, let us speak once more about Andrei Tarkovsky. During the Locarno film festival in August 1972, I met him in person when he was chair of the judges considering my film, *Stella da Falla*, the Swiss competition entry. This was his first longer trip to the West, and his own film, *Andrei Rublev*, was showing at the Piazza Grande. He caught sight of me from the other end of the large festival hall, and asked his Russian-speaking attendant whether the person he was looking at (me) was indeed the director of the film shown the day before. He nodded towards me, and we approached each other tentatively to shake hands. Before the prize was announced he was forbidden from talking to filmmakers.[73] There are grounds to believe however that he was at least interested in *Stella da Falla*, connected with his comment, cited earlier: '*Whether or not a director possesses depth becomes apparent in his reasons for shooting films. How he does this and the method he employs is entirely beside the point...*'[74]

The conditions under which our two films, both shown at Locarno, were made, were no doubt entirely different. Tarkovsky had undertaken a long training at the VGIK, the Soviet Institute of Cinematography in Moscow, which approached filmmaking with Socialist intent (and he was extremely critical of it until the end of his life). I was a 22-year-old, self-taught filmmaker who had created *Stella da Falla* the year previously with a film crew thrown haphazardly together. This was during a year in which I travelled through all of western Europe in a VW bus, staying for short intervals at a farm commune in Toggenburg.

Yet there were points of accord, such as my endorsement of the following two statements:

> External motion sequences, intrigues, concatenations of events, do not interest me in the least, less and less so from film to film. I am most preoccupied with the human being's inner world, within which the universe is encompassed. And to explore this

idea, to be able to give expression to the meaning of human life, truly requires no external chain of events.[75]

The purity of film, and its untranslatable power, becomes apparent not, say, in the symbolic acuity of its images, however keen these may be, but in the tangible specificity and the unrepeatability of the images which give expression to a fact of reality.[76]

Tarkovsky turned against film sequences that sought to be *symbolically meaningful*, favouring instead an accentuation of actuality in a composed, spiritual context.[77] In my view, he offended against this basic principle in his last films, presenting as real fiction, which no filmed dream ought to be, a dream world whose enigmatic images all move or strive beyond the sensory reality they depict. This moved Ingmar Bergman to utter the following praise: 'For me, Tarkovsky is the most important because he has found a language that corresponds to the intrinsic nature of film: life as a dream.'

Thus some praise the affinity of Tarkovsky's film to dream life, while others (including Tarkovsky himself) emphasize a 'human realism', an ability to 'freeze real time'. In Bergman's films, when the protagonist's dreams are inserted into the action (as in *Wild Strawberries*), the viewer is not left in the dark about the form of consciousness represented in the sequence of images. Tarkovsky, on the other hand (and David Lynch imitates him in this), insists on erasing and obscuring transitions from a documented sensory occurrence to memories or fantasies and dreams connected with them, so as to benefit the unity of work he seeks. Depending on our predisposition as viewers this may either grip or alienate us. 'Life as a dream' then suggests almost complete elimination of the independent meaning of a recorded external world. Thus surrealist or 'poetic film sequences' (Tarkovsky himself rejected this designation for his films) aim to fulfil the function of expressing nothing but inner soul experience.

The first and last shots in Tarkovsky's film *Sacrifice*, which show the watering of a dried-up tree, are not intended as some kind of gardening tip but, as Tarkovsky writes, are a 'metaphor for belief'.[78] Here we can recall Béla Balázs and his words about the 'redemption of outer reality from the chaos of the random and transient'. Tarkovsky, as a student at the Moscow Film School, started from this naturalistic, documenting approach; and, for instance in *The Mirror*, was able to enhance its use to striking and compelling effect.

In speaking of Lumière's *The Arrival of the Train* (see note 72), Tarkovsky adds:

> A new aesthetic principle arose here, consisting of the fact that, for the first time in the history of art and culture, it was found possible to directly 'fix' time, and at the same time to reproduce it as often as desired, or in other words to keep returning to it. In this way the human being gained a matrix of *real time*. Time surveyed and fixed could now be stored for a long time (and theoretically for ever) in metal containers.[79]

This potential is employed in films such as Tarkovsky's *The Mirror*, by borrowing shots from a Russian film archive showing the march of Soviet soldiers through the seemingly endless shallow waters of Lake Sivash in Crimea. The cameraman, who was killed the next day, had taken unusually lengthy footage to record this single, precise observation of his comrades.

Andrei Tarkovsky (1932–1986) Photo © RIA Novosti

Similarly, in my film, *Stella da Falla*, I used three contemporary film documents from the turn of the nineteenth to twentieth centuries. The hero, who has fallen from medieval times into the present, buys an 8mm film camera and says to the person selling it:

> Is this the kind of machine that when, sometimes you see something that is eerily beautiful, and then it's gone again, you can turn this kind of apparatus upon what you see and press some button somewhere, and then you have it all inside here on a film? And then you can look at it again and again, as often as you like. Is that right?
>
> *The seller:* Yes, that's a film camera.[80]

Well, the art of film cannot consist in naturalistic, inflationary reproduction of random occurrences caught on camera without any connection with the unity of the film. It lives, rather, from an artistic reshaping or remoulding governed by a higher artistic sense. Tarkovsky says: '*Observation* is the fundamental, formative element in cinema, pervading and determining it from the most insignificant-seeming pictorial detail onward.'[81] And then, emphasizing the 'fiction' of an artistically realized observation, he goes on: 'Fixing of naturalistic facts is not nearly sufficient for creating a filmic scene. Cinematic image is founded on a capacity to present one's own feeling of an object as *observation*.'[82] This means that, in Tarkovsky's sense, a cinematic image is not immediately present in the content of a sensory reality caught on camera. An outer content of observation should unite with its imaginative, inner 'interpretation' by transformation into something 'observed'. To make clear what he meant, Tarkovsky undertook various efforts in the field of film theory and analysis. Studying them shows that, while they contain stimulating discoveries, they also sometimes reveal the vague and provisional nature of his conceptual clarifications.

When Novalis notes to himself, 'The more philosophical, the more poetical', this comment is illumined by the entire corpus of his profound and universal aesthetic fragments.[83] Tarkovsky writes as follows: 'Only when the film director presents his own view of

things* and thus becomes a kind of philosopher, is he also in fact an artist, and cinematography becomes an art of film. But he is a philosopher only in a very limited sense. It is high time to recall the comment by Paul Valéry: 'Poets – philosophers! This is the same as confusing the painter of seascapes with a ship's captain.' A genuine film artist, says Tarkovsky, is also a philosopher, but we should not confuse philosophy with art. This essayistic remark is intended to suggest in very general terms that the question of truth and meaning also plays a central role for the film director. And yet he ought not to dig down too deep for otherwise he probably won't make films any more. In other words, he will no longer paint seascapes. (Or does the artist, rather, occupy the position of captain in Valéry's image? Such indeterminacies always arise when metaphors possess no experiential basis in soul observation.) Goethe may have felt similarly when he made the following remark after visiting Schelling:

> I would go to see him often if I did not still hope for poetic moments; and philosophy disrupts poetry within me, probably because it drives me into objectivity. I can never maintain my

---

* In the previous sentence this view was equated with 'his own thought system' and 'his deepest dreams' — author's note.

speculative stance but must immediately seek tangible perception, and therefore I flee straight out into nature.

Rudolf Steiner quotes this comment in his book, *Goethe's Worldview*,[84] and then continues: 'He was not able to find the highest perception, that of the world of ideas itself. This cannot destroy poetry, for it liberates the spirit from all conjectures that something unknown, unfathomable could exist in nature.' [What is unknown and unfathomable manifests solely within us.]

That Tarkovsky wished to maintain an indeterminate stance towards his own formulated concepts meant that some of his films contradict his own theories of film. 'In art', he wrote, 'a person appropriates reality through subjective experience. In science, human knowledge follows the steps of an endless staircase, with ever new insights into the world replacing old ones.'[85] Here we are confronted with a somewhat uninspiring choice: either I cultivate my subjective experience as if it were the only reality, or I follow the endless footsteps of scientific paths that never touch solid ground. In this case we can resort only to the shallow comfort of Godard, which we here recall, according to which, "[cinematic] depiction consoles us for the sadness of life. Life consoles us for the fact that depiction is nothing."

Tarkovsky's neglect of the common root of art and science led him with increasing age to ever more abstract societal complaints, both against the 'commercial West' and against his own authoritarian regime in the USSR, and similarly against the Moscow film school that he had attended for many years. He was unable to jettison the humanist cultural ballast preventing him from penetrating to 'perception of the world of ideas' that cannot destroy poetry. Thus he took refuge in an artistic morality in which sacrifice and magic play a central part. This expressed itself in films in which the externalized flow of time, transformed through strenuous artistic efforts into a 'matrix of real time', unites with expression of the 'deepest dreams', of 'nostalgia' (the title of one of his last films) — that is, the memory of subjective privations — to create a cipher of human existence.

By the end, Tarkovsky was increasingly taking a polemical stand against himself on various fronts:

> 'Poetical film'* is now a pretty worn out idea. We mean by it the kind of film whose images boldly overstep the factual tangibility of real life and at the same time constitute a separate constructive unity. This conceals a special danger — that of the cinema here growing distant from itself. The poetical film usually produces symbols, allegories and similar rhetorical figures. And it is precisely these that in fact have nothing in common with the kind of pictorial quality that constitutes the nature of cinema.[86]

Without citing examples, he turns against poetry in cinema that 'oversteps the factual tangibility of real life', though this must appear quite incomprehensible if we think of Tarkovsky's own later films, which largely dispense with any references to the 'factual tangibility of real life'.

Another term of key importance for Tarkovsky, that of freedom, remains vague and ambivalent:

> Today we all possess the characteristic trait of an unbelievable egoism. But it is not in this that freedom lies. It lies, rather, in us having to learn at last to demand nothing of life or our fellow human beings but only of ourselves. This is the offering of sacrifice in the name of love.[87]

We could agree with this both in general and in particular if Tarkovsky would characterize even a single instance of what he describes as a genuine 'sacrifice in the name of love'. In connection with it he refers to our endurance of 'endless constraints', saying that this is what should mark the creative person. The capacity to put up with constraints? Surely this is an unimportant aspect of freedom, which sometimes figures in connection with it.

> I do not understand how artists can speak of absolute creative freedom. Those who embark on the path of creativity, fall into the grip of endless constraints that bind them to their tasks,

---

* which Pasolini used in his quest for an art of film — author's note.

their destiny as an artist. Everything and everyone is bound by constraints.[88]

Here Tarkovsky is attacking his prime enemy, the 'commercial film', which stands in an 'unequal struggle with the art of film'. In his view, the ideological 'freedom' of the West to be able to see all the films of famous directors — something he so badly missed in the Soviet Union when he was young — cannot prevent the decline of 'cinematic art'. And why not? Because, according to Tarkovsky, the fundamentally suggestive function of cinema, its 'magical effect', which we have mentioned a great deal in connection with Steiner's characterizations of the medium, serves both the 'commercial cinema' *and* 'cinematic art'.

And how does Tarkovsky distinguish the one from the other?

> The specific effects of cinema (in other words the equivalence between film and life), are such that even the brashest commercial blockbuster can exert the same magical effect on an uncritical public as the true art of film has on a discerning cinema-goer. The decisive, and indeed tragic difference lies in the fact that an artistic film wakens emotions and thoughts in its audience whereas blockbusters, with their very appealing and irresistible effect, actually irreversibly extinguish the last thoughts and feelings of their audiences. People who no longer have any need for beauty and the spirit, use film like a bottle of Coca-Cola.

This black-and-white verdict can be understood only in the context of a more or less religious attachment to cultural humanism, which, in the words of Pasolini, conflicts with a developing awareness of futurity.[89] It runs the risk of overlooking the imperfect nature of an instinctive creativity and thereby unintentionally nurturing a cult of genius that paralyses the schooling of artistic awareness.

> Film is the only art in which an author can feel himself to be the creator of a limitless reality, of a literally unique world. The innate tendency in us to affirm ourselves is most comprehensively and directly realized in the cinema above all. Film is an emotional reality, and the viewer thus also absorbs it as a second reality. Film directing is therefore literally the capacity 'to separate the light

from the darkness, the waters from dry land'. This possibility creates the illusion that allows the director to see himself as a demiurge.[90]

Thus over-valuation of 'creation' becomes apparent as an aesthetic imbalance between Expressionist and Impressionist means of composition. As we heard, Tarkovsky favours the first, and thus he is unreceptive to the artistic quality of tellingly Impressionist narrative structures. 'Narrative' seems for him to mean nothing more than 'costume dramas' as 'audience manipulation' for purely commercial reasons, thus mere 'entertainment'. But it is significant that we cannot make general statements as to what is entertaining and what is not. Someone who buys a cinema ticket is certainly not going to see a film in order *not* to be entertained.

> A truly artistic idea is always something that torments the artist, indeed, can be almost life-threatening. Its realization can be compared only with a decisive and momentous step in life. It has always been so, for all who engaged with art. And yet sometimes we can have the sense that we are preoccupied today more or less only with retelling ancient stories — as if our audience were coming to us as to a grandmother, with her headscarf and knitting needles, and we were entertaining it with fairytales of all kinds. A story may have an entertaining and diverting quality, yet it is nothing but idle chit-chat, helping an audience to pass the time.[91]

An 'entertaining film' will very probably not entertain all who see it. But why should we not be entertained by a Tarkovsky film, at least if he succeeds in concealing any signs of the 'tormenting' or even 'almost life-threatening' quality that was, for him, connected with making the film?

Tarkovsky must anyway have been well aware of fairytales as an outstanding instance of narrative sequences that treat of non-sensory spiritual things without recourse to dreams and visions! Is it perhaps possible that Tarkovsky failed to take note of significant works of narrative film that were shown in the cinemas of his day, simply because they were produced in America? I am thinking for instance of films that were showing everywhere in the 70s: *The Godfather*, 1 and 2 by Francis Ford Coppola (1972 and 74), *The Conversation* (1974), likewise by Coppola, *Chinatown* (1974) by Roman Polanski, *Taxi Driver* (1976) by Martin Scorsese, *The Deer Hunter* (1976) by Michael Cimino, etc.

'As opposed to common assumptions, art's functional calling is not to stimulate thoughts or mediate ideas, or serve as example. No, the goal of art, rather, is to prepare us for our death, to affect and move us in our deepest inner being...'[92] Modern spirituality can only be founded on cognition, just as art, if it is to be a positive force in the future, must be founded on knowledge and perception. It avoids the personal pathos that conceives of death as a trial for which art should prepare us. The idea of death — there is no other option for the living — is of little importance since physical death merely concludes the dying process that occurs throughout life. It was Rudolf Steiner's intention to use film to invoke imaginative experience of the laws of destiny and reincarnation, so as to support in the viewer perception of how this present life passes away to create the germinal foundation for a life in the future. What 'affects and moves us in our deepest inner being' is something that such films would leave to matters of personal destiny — as in the case also of Andrei Tarkovsky's own life.

12

In his latter years, Andrei Tarkovsky studied the works of Rudolf Steiner with keen interest. He made various efforts to find all the books and lecture series that had ever been translated into Russian. I invited him to visit me if he were ever to think of making a film about Rudolf Steiner's life. At that time I was still living in Dornach, the most important location of Steiner's work after Berlin. In the last two years of his life, already gravely ill with cancer, he considered various film projects. One concerned 'the life of saints', as his friends in Paris reported. Another project, as his son Andrei Tarkovsky junior related, concerned the life of Judas Iscariot.

Two years before his death he came to Berlin with the German film director and media academic Alexander Kluge, and tried living there for a while. He suggested to Kluge a joint film project based on essays Steiner wrote between 1904 and 1908, which were later collected under the title *From the Akashic Records*. The interview with Kluge in 2012 that related to this,[93] referred to various points of disagreement about it between the two directors. I will raise one of these points here since it seems to me to involve basic principles of cinematic art:

> *Interviewer:* How could one conceive of the relationship between merely visible things and an invisible, supersensible realm within the medium of cinematography? It seems that camera recording might contradict a form of spiritual or supersensible vision.

This question, of how a poetic, imaginative content could inform the medium of film and its rigid naturalism, was something that Kluge then approached from various angles:

> *Alexander Kluge:* I'm not sure. You were speaking about reality, which is, if you like, the convention of our senses which, via

other people's senses, we adapt to what we think we see or hear — which we use as the outer skin of our experience. In my view it's like this: the camera here possesses what one might call a 'visual unconscious'. That's an expression coined by Walter Benjamin. The camera registers something that runs counter to our habitual way of seeing, and we are then astonished at what we see. The camera has, as it were, slipped in under our structure of attention. That is one aspect. The other is that a film engenders a third image, as it were, in the montage between two others. You see something that strikes you, and as this impression is still unfolding, another image appears, contrasting with it. In the gap where there is nothing, where, if you like there exists only the contradiction between two shots, a third picture arises in the viewer's thought. We can call this epiphany. This epiphany is the basic form of the intimating capacity. Every esotericist knows that epiphany enables us to see through things and beyond them...

In this interview, in which Kluge ranks himself with the esotericists, he answers the initial question with a very hazy distinction between 'sensory reality' and technically reproducible perception (to which a 'visual unconscious' attaches), and then refers to film montage which seeks to conjure a spiritual context in the viewer through the 'third picture' that he himself engenders (as 'epiphany').

Let us take a closer look at Kluge's 'third picture'. The viewer is compelled to form a subconscious picture — not an unconscious one as Kluge says — as long as he seeks to attend to the film for his entertainment or for some other reason. The screenplay has already planned in the sensory bridge between two images as anticipation of Kluge's 'third picture', and the audience has largely become accustomed to the conventional modes of film-mediated scenarios. It is no longer the case, as was reported in the era of silent movies, that gentlemen occupy the front seats in the cinema because they have heard about the scene with the pretty young lady in the bathtub. Nor is it necessary nowadays to fade in intermediate captions such as 'some years later' or employ a dimming cross-dissolve to indicate that a memory or dream is to follow.

If a film is not made as a one-take movie (which, as 'fake documentary' of a unified occurrence, requires no context over and above the sensory material presented),[94] and if the viewer is not presented with a collage of random film snippets, he will take up the idea of contextuality embedded in the cut, and envisaged in the screenplay, which Kluge unsatisfactorily calls the 'third picture'; or, if he does not access this idea, will content himself with the context that he himself creates through his own thought.

Kluge describes the material of cinematic art as recorded visual and auditory impression which the camera's recording alters such that its reproduction runs counter to the 'customary gaze'. The camera, he says, brings to light a 'visual unconscious'. Here we must distinguish two factors: one lies in the recording technique we have repeatedly mentioned which becomes manifest in a subconscious, physiological compulsion. It compels us to picture movements where in reality there is only a swift succession of single still images. It does not matter here whether we have single photographic shots (film) or digital additions of image pixels (TV+digital cinema).

The second factor, that enables something to 'slip in under the structure of attention', consists in the absence of an emotional intentionality that always inheres in our 'customary gaze'. The 'natural gaze' focuses on particular areas of the visual field, or equally can intentionally defocus. The film image, on the other hand, if shots do not imitate our natural focus through continuous redefinition, leaves the viewer free to choose his own focus as he wishes in the overall scenario (though quick movement sequences in the centre of our visual field in turn strongly run counter to that freedom). If we're driving through a tunnel, for example, in expectation of the other end of the tunnel, our 'natural', instinctive gaze focuses usually on a small section in front of the bonnet, whereas a film image shot with a wider angle from the same position will also include wave movements of the tunnel lights whizzing past the edge of vision, which, in Kluge's terms, belong to our 'visual unconscious'.

The formal techniques of cinematic art assign a central role to the cutting, sequencing and juxtaposition of shots (though Tarkovsky, as we will see, disputes this). Film montage is the means to direct the flow of the viewer's thoughts in a way that serves the cinematic idea. Since almost all cinematic ideas consist of stories with happy, tragic or sometimes open-ended outcomes,[95] cuts serve to sharpen and abbreviate the narrative.

As we saw, for Rudolf Steiner the inartistic nature of cinema lay, among other things, in the fact that transitions facilitated by cuts remain empty, since created by purely technical means. He expressed this as follows:

> Setting something into external motion can never create a musical mood. And modern civilization offers proof that it is unmusical by reaching for drastic methods. It really is true to say that, in its secret inner soul, modern civilization has sought to provide the clearest proof of its lack of musicality, and has done so by developing film. Cinema is the clearest proof that someone who loves it is unmusical, since film is founded on according inner validity only to what does not rise up from within the soul but is, rather, initiated from without.[96]

In other words, a musical context arises through an inner activity of soul that is activated in 'sensory interstices' between recall of the tone that has just resounded and intimating anticipation of how subsequent auditory impressions will figure in the contrary interweaving of past and future. In this lecture on tone eurythmy, Rudolf Steiner presented to his listeners the surprising definition of music as being 'what one does not hear'. Any astonishment at such a remark can be modified by the easily gained insight that experience of a melody is based on its intervals, that is, on seven (or twelve) different forms of tonal transition accomplished partly also by the person listening to musical works. Where inner musical grasp of objectively determined (thus not listener-dependent) transitional qualities of the intervals is lacking, the acoustic impression will be of a lower order than music, even if the listener should have outstanding hearing.[97]

Wolf Otto Pfeiffer, initiator of the Berlin Film Spirit Association,[98] writes: ' "Dramaturgy" assumes that a film is what we see on the screen. The basic assumption of "poetology", on the other hand, is that the decisive thing is not what we see in a film but what we do not see.'[99] In saying this, he is seeking a spiritualization or we could also say an inner musicalization of cinema. He is urging us to make films that prompt enhanced activity by film consumers precisely by offering 'interstices' that they themselves must actively fill.

Tarkovsky, as we saw, turned against 'classical montage' as this was taught for decades at the VGIK, the Moscow film school, based on Russian film pioneers such as Eisenstein. He presented well-founded objections. He pointed out how inartistic it is to try to create tension and involvement solely through mechanical rhythm and acceleration of the cut cadence, supported by a sensory, sensual impetus. His critique can be substantiated in relation to thousands of action scenes. Here, what Tarkovsky criticized in regard to some of Eisenstein's films applies too to cinema-goers who find this 'clumsy' stylistic approach, typical of film, to be entertaining:

> Despite the lightning-rapid flare of shots, the unprejudiced viewer, at least, will not be unaware of the aridity and unnatural-ness of the process unfolding on screen. The shots remain extremely static and vapid. And thus a contradiction naturally arises between the inner content of a film shot, which does not retain any kind of temporal process, and the rapidity of the montage, which is entirely artificial, external and indifferent to the time that elapses in the shot.[100]

In the famously long shots in Tarkovsky's late works — comparable in this to Antonioni — the viewer has an experience of the specific 'time pressure of a shot'.

> These shots are, as one says, not mountable, that is, they are not easily sequenced in periodicities that are fundamentally divergent. Just as little as, say, waterpipes with different dia-meters. The temporal coherence running through one shot, the growing or evaporating tension of time, is what we call the *time pressure* within a shot. Accordingly, montage involves uniting parts of film in a way that takes account of the time pressure at work in them.[101]

> It is hard to agree with the view that montage is the most important, formative element in a film, and that the film as it were is created on the cutting and montage table.

Though I have always seen cutting as the most interesting task in making a film — in so far as it can be compared not with collage but with composition — its scope is limited by the available material. Its importance does indeed recede if the prime focus, as in Tarkovsky, shifts to a shaping of the pictorial contents of separate shots, and if this is favoured over the multiplying possibilities of bringing each one 'into conversation' with others.

> Montage only coordinates already occupied shots, structuring from them the living organism of the film in whose blood vessels the time that guarantees its living function pulses with a rhythmically variable pressure.[102]

> A coordination of temporally unequal shots leads inevitably to a break in rhythm. If this was, however, prepared for by the inner life of the coordinated shots, it can certainly prove to be indispensable for the necessary rhythmic picture. We need think here only of the different possible forms of temporal pressure-tension, in symbolic terms the differences between brook, stream, river, waterfall and ocean. Their coordination creates a unique rhythmic painting, an organic innovation brought to life by its author's sense of temporality. In my view, a director who can, without more ado, montage his films in many diverse ways, is anything other than profound.[103]

With his idea of the 'individual rhythmic picture', Tarkovsky touches on a unique aspect of the individual human spirit whose ongoing evolution can only proceed in the greatest of all conceivable rhythms, that is, in recurring embodiments or incarnations. In his sense of individualized picture rhythms, he subconsciously touches on one aspect (reincarnation) of Rudolf Steiner's specific intentions for film. Tarkovsky has less interest in the other side of the coin, the workings of destiny as a filmic idea: his relativization of montage also gives expression to a certain antipathy towards filmic narrative. 'True narrative' however is what forms the basis for presenting viewers with the sway of karmic laws in cinematic experience.[104]

Tarkovsky may perhaps leave too much unclear in relation to the magical effect he seeks for cinematic scenarios, equating them vaguely with an individual 'quest for time' by the filmmaker.

> In film, rhythm emerges organically, corresponding to the sense of life innate in its director, according to his quest for time. It even seems to me that time in the shot must unfold independently and with its own dignity. Only then do ideas find a place without over-hasty restlessness. The feeling for rhythm is the same as — let us say — intuiting the right word in literature. An imprecise word in literature destroys the truthful character of a work in the same way that an imprecise rhythm does in film.[105]

The comparison with literature is an apt one for Tarkovsky, who uses many literary means to create room for 'ideas in the tranquility of filmic motion paintings'. Associated with this, however, as we have already indicated, is the danger of erasing the specific nature of cinematic art. It is this also that gave rise to dispute between Kluge and Tarkovsky. Kluge criticized Tarkovsky for his search for a magically charged image, which drew on his experience of icons, at odds with Kluge's view of film. In the conversation quoted, Kluge mentions in this context the Byzantine dispute about images in the eighth and ninth centuries, which was concerned with the meaning and importance of icons. The theologians of the time were asking this central question: is the icon a pictorial pointer towards knowledge geared only to a pictureless supersensible reality, or is it itself a spiritual reality capable of clothing itself in sensory earthly nature? Thus fierce disputes arose between the iconodules (picture lovers) and the iconoclasts (picture haters). (An ideologically more rigid recurrence of this dispute was expressed around eight hundred years later in the conflict between Protestants and Catholics.)

Here is a further excerpt from Fagard's interview with Kluge:[106]

> *Interviewer:* So would you be more interested in non-images?
>
> *Alexander Kluge:* That can't be said so generally. You can't create non-images without having images. But images allow us to look

through them: epiphany.[107] If we reflect on light, it is not possible to say that it unquestionably involves an image.

Interviewer: Exactly. Light would be the source of an image.

Alexander Kluge: The source of the image as the path of all images; and at the same time it appears transparent, diaphanous. If you look at a sunbeam, it is very bright, clear, and superior to what it brings to sight.

Kluge was pointing to the spiritual nature of all picture-forming powers, and saying that all sensory images are subordinate to their originating source. In grasping naturally given sense images we experience the end results of the evolution which underlies both the formation of the human body and the whole cosmos. Creatures perceive themselves in their naturalness, that is, in the connecting dependency of their creaturehood. The film image is the outcome of a mechanical-chemical process, or, in currently employed technology, of a fine-mechanical electronic one, whose underlying representations employ a physical lens system. In the works of painters, the picture-shaping powers activated in the mind of the painter are made directly manifest through a brush in form and colour; and this means that in the materials of paintings that, as it were, become transparent to form, whether by Rublev, Giotto, Raphael, Dürer, Carpaccio (whom Tarkovsky loved so much), van Eyck, Vermeer, Rembrandt, Bosch through to Redon, Monet and Gauguin, and all the others, we also become aware of the picture-forming powers at work in the painterly imagination of their originators. Since the human being does not participate in the emergence of the material basis of film images, Tarkovsky's intention 'to make space for ideas in the filmic image' continues to require explanation.

I hope it has become clear that it is not a matter either of religious veneration of images nor of contempt for them, but rather, as in all critique of art, of distinguishing between appearance that is 'good' or 'not good'. In all art, the engendering process of configuration manifests in images, whether via words and rhythms, melodies and harmonies, colours and forms, or dance movements and dance positions. All of these arise from imagelessness and vanish into it again in the mind of the reflective observer. The artistic source is individual, that is, connected with the artist's soul-spiritual experience of himself. Thus images, also unintentionally, reflect his self-feeling and the self-awareness he has achieved. Even when a 'traditional' artist still relies on the existence of a subconscious Muse or creative source, expressing this nevertheless bears the signature of his conscious efforts to bring what is subconscious to light.[108]

In the much-quoted chapter 'On Time, Rhythm and Editing' in his book, *Sculpting in Time: Reflections on the Cinema*, Tarkovsky opposes both Eisenstein's and Kluge's theories of film as follows:

> The intention of the representatives of 'montage cinema', whereby editing creates two concepts that as it were produce a third, seems to me also to stand in stark contrast with the nature of cinema itself. Playing with concepts cannot ultimately be the goal of art. When Pushkin said that 'poetry must be somewhat simple', he was probably thinking of the tangibility of the material element that inheres in an image which, in mysterious, magical fashion, strives toward spheres of spirit.

This is a further indication that Tarkovsky was not really able to clarify his yearning for pictorial spiritual experiences, which therefore had to remain an unfulfilled longing. Whenever he speaks of the 'magic' of images, often equating film images with painterly ones, we see his instinctive familiarity with the spiritual world of imagination at work. Ideas, as they manifest in individual thinking experience, are of course not founded on electrochemical brain processes but on the bearer of the 'sense of time' that Tarkovsky places at the centre of his film art. This is the lowest aspect of our spiritual organization, which we can term the life body, etheric body, or body of formative forces etc., and which we discussed earlier in reference to Steiner's comment about becoming 'etherically saucer-eyed'.

> But how do we experience the time quality of a shot? This sense arises when a certain significant truth becomes palpable behind the visible occurrence. Then we clearly and palpably perceive

that what we see in this shot is not fully accounted for by visual representation but only intimates something that spreads out infinitely beyond it, and points us to *life*...[109]

Even though the German translation* of Tarkovsky's texts is sometimes questionable, this does not affect the fact that Tarkovsky, when he's trying to point to a purely inner experience, often purports to be describing a typical cinematic experience. This relates to his difficulty in overcoming Leninist materialism, a physicalism of worldview, with which he was imbued as he was growing up in the Soviet Union, and which hindered his access to a spiritual science without such preconceptions.

We will end our thoughts on appearance and essence, on archetypes and reflected images, by restating a conviction that whatever artform is involved will be concerned not with unreal appearance within sensory reality but with the manifestation of a higher reality within the unreality of mere sense appearance. By acknowledging this we can take our leave from materialistic ideas that today pervade not only people's perceptions of art, thus aesthetics, but all disciplines, as a global superstition that the structuring principles of the universe are devoid of spirit (atoms, black holes, background radiation, antimatter etc.).[110]

Even if the early, crass form of nineteenth century materialism has been superseded, it still retains ideological supremacy in state-directed centres of higher education in the form of unquestioned assumptions about psychophysical parallelism. No one today would still defend the statement made by the Paris physiologist, Cabani at the beginning of the nineteenth century, that 'The brain produces thoughts as the liver produces bile'. And yet the modern ideas of many scientists in the fields of medicine, biology and physiology, if taken to their logical conclusion, scarcely differ really from those of Cabani.

---

* Translator's note: The passages from Tarkovsky's works have been translated into English from the German version.

This is the only way to explain why the results of experiments undertaken by the physiologist, Libet, starting in 1979, and repeated throughout the world in various psychology labs, are still cited today even though the experimental model appears to anyone who scrutinizes it carefully to be highly dubious in terms of the formulated goal of research. At any rate, Libet interpreted his time measurements such that 'the decision to act is made by unconscious brain processes before it enters consciousness as an intention; thus conscious decision-making is not the cause of action.'[111] In other words, before we decide to act, the brain has long since decided for us in advance. We can therefore be regarded merely as the functionary or civil servant of our own brain.

The example of the connection between thinking and the brain, as this figures in countless numbers of unnecessary books on the subject, can bring home to us the fundamental error of a materialism bent on defending its spirit blindness. Coercive causalities, referred to as 'natural laws', are studied as the sole constituting principles of the world, within whose framework the human being is assigned a marginal, miniature observer role within a gigantic and purely physical cosmos.

This intrinsically spirit-devoid cosmic machinery, the supposedly sole cause of death of individual creatures, is at odds with a spiritual science emancipated from preconceptions and limits to knowledge, which opens the gaze to a transformed view of the world as renewed by the activity of individual human spirits. In this view there are, in principle, no problems with integrating all the separate findings of classical science into an overarching idea of human and world evolution.

The following, simplified account of the outlook of spiritual science may be of service here to those unfamiliar with such thinking: the essence of a concept or idea does *not* lie in a biochemical brain process accompanied by firing neurons, which materialism regards as the cause of emotional and mental experience. The connection between our ever-increasing knowledge of neurocerebral processes in recent years[112] and individual cognitive activity, can only be discovered by the latter (it seems almost embarrassing to even mention this). Understanding the connection that does, without doubt, exist between thinking activity and its manifestation in physical brain processes, is thus not gained from studying cerebral activity but by means of the ideas which, in the inner observation of thinking experience, completely permeate outer sensory observations involving brain processes.

As long ago as the last decade of the nineteenth century, in his enquiries into this dynamic, Rudolf Steiner discovered that parallel cerebral processes during more or less conscious thinking activity enable the human individual to have a kind of reflection of the free activity of his spiritual being, which the latter needs in order to acquire self-awareness within ordinary daily consciousness.[113] The form of activity of the body-free, world-connected human entelechy, that of perceiving thinking, would remain alien to itself within the inner personal soul if it could not encounter itself in recallable outcomes of its activity in thoughts 'dulled' or 'dimmed' by means of cerebral engrams.[114] Rudolf Steiner described this process as follows in his *The Philosophy of Freedom* (1894):

> From this we can see how thinking finds its counterpart in our bodily organization. And if we recognize this, we will no longer be able to misapprehend the importance of this counterpart for thinking itself. When we walk over soft ground, our feet leave footprints in it. We will not be tempted to say that these footprints have been pushed up from below by the forces of the earth. We will not ascribe to <u>these</u> forces an active part in creating the footprints. In the same way, if we observe the nature of thinking without preconception, we will not ascribe to its traces in the bodily organism a part that is played by virtue of the fact that thinking prepares its emergence through the body.[115]

In this process neither the essential I nor its expression in self-aware, intentional thinking remain bound to the cerebral mirroring function. This mirroring function can also be taken over by higher, spiritually developed organs of perception within the overall human entity, by overcoming and emancipating ourselves from our sense- and brain-bound nature.[116]

13

In early periods of cultural development as far as we can ascertain it through historical documents, artworks arose in connection with centres of cultural life located in Sumerian, Egyptian and Greek temples. Here, religious life was cultivated as sacred connection with the world of spirit and its divine inhabitants. Specific details of this become apparent from, among other sources, the testimonies of ancient European narratives such as the Gilgamesh epic, with its Sumerian gods, and the Homeric epics with their vision of the gods drawn from Greek mystery centres (such as Eleusis and Ephesus) and the destinies of heroic figures such as Achilles or Odysseus. The earliest western European romances are founded on the Christian mystery of the Grail, in the same way that Japanese haiku are based on Zen schooling, Raphael's paintings are underpinned by Catholic theology, and Goethe's *Faust* is predicated on a battle with the devil.

Passing through stages of loss of spiritual perception and experience, evolution descended successively into psychologizing forms of expression of an ever more subjective nature, down to existentialist, nihilist or socialist interpretations of daily life. Only at these spiritually restricted and constrained levels of reflection, did artistic inventiveness and creativity come to self-awareness. It emancipated itself from the residual glimmers of a dreamlike, visionary spiritual perception, which increasingly faded away into rigidified faith (*credo quia absurdum*)[117], thence into diluted channels of moral humanism and finally into 'enlightened' and ever-adaptable forms of bourgeois comfort. In the end phase of religious emancipation that characterizes our era, the ship of the arts ran aground on arbitrariness, as can be confirmed by any unprejudiced or independent glance at the art world today.

Film art arose at an evolutionary stage of fragmenting sub-jectivity, as a materialistic culmination. The chief protagonists presented in the most successful films are — as we saw earlier — often either psychopaths (Hannibal Lecter & Co.) or unbelievable heroes (Superman & Co.). Film directors and film producers respond to the spiritually weak and inarticulate needs of their audiences, or educate them to be so; and it is therefore hardly surprising that the development of a true art of film keeps coming up against both inner and outer impediments. Novalis was already aware of this dynamic, and a visionary precursor in the quest to recapture artistic creativity. He noted in a diary: 'For the ancients, religion was in a sense what it ought to become for us: practical poetry.' It seemed to Novalis that this 'practical poetry' only had meaning in connection with a modern, fully conscious spiritual perception.[118]

Rudolf Steiner's idea of an art of film has the finest connection with the developmental trajectory urged by Novalis. His research, practice and enactment of artistic forces in both the spatial and temporal arts is founded on a renewal of the spiritual consciousness of reality. Often, and in ever new guises, he showed how new narrative materials and perspectives can be found by deepening true self-knowledge. In forthcoming decades and centuries, with increasing validity and inevitability, a sustaining self-knowledge founded upon world knowledge and no longer on academic psychologies, will come to encompass an awareness of reincarnation and destiny.

In western evolution, the fact of individual spiritual freedom was first described in its evolutionary and transpersonal significance by German Idealists and classicists (Fichte, Hegel, Schelling, Lessing, Goethe, Schiller, Novalis et al.). To prevent this new evolutionary impulse of spiritual freedom succumbing to blind egoism, the individual will seek to defend it as a spiritually objective process by resisting consciousness-dimming impulses of sensory habit. This is, as we know, because both crass and subtle egoism are founded on an accentuation of self-awareness without the real presence of spirit.

In one of his last letters to the members of the Anthroposophical Society,[119] Rudolf Steiner described this evolutionary context in detail. I want to quote a longer passage from the end of the letter since it can, if we understand it, answer many of the questions so far thrown up in these pages in grand and panoramic fashion.

> The possibility for us to develop freedom lies in the fact that, in our momentary *thinking*, we live not in reality but only a reflection of reality, in pictorial existence. All existence in our consciousness is compelling. Only the *picture* cannot act with compulsion. If something is to happen as a result of the impression made by it, this must happen quite independently *of the picture itself*. We become free by virtue of the fact that we raise ourselves with our consciousness soul out of reality and surface in the *non-reality* of picture.
>
> And here the important question arises: do we not lose reality when part of our being departs from this reality, and we throw ourselves into non-reality?
>
> Here once again is the point where we meet one of the great enigmas in our observation of the world.
>
> What is experienced in thinking arose from the cosmos. In relation to the cosmos we throw ourselves into non-reality. In thinking we *liberate* ourselves from all the powers of the cosmos. We paint the cosmos which we stand outside of.
>
> If this was all that we did, freedom would light up in us for a cosmic moment; but in the same moment our human nature would dissolve. But as we become free from the cosmos in thinking, we are still attached in our unconscious soul life to our past lives on earth and our lives between death and rebirth. As conscious human being we are in picture existence, while our unconscious resides in spiritual reality. While we experience freedom in our *present* I, our *past* I retains us in reality.

Rudolf Steiner's intention was to focus on our subconscious connection with our former lives on earth through pictures, that is, in cinematic images. Naturally this would not be in the form of doctrinal treatise but would employ the specific means of cinematic art, which, as we have heard, he considered suitable for this theme. If such a thing were to succeed,[120] the imagination of the screenplay author and the director would need to be emancipated from arbitrary fantasy. Only then could it convincingly portray, in its scenes and situations, the reality of its protagonists' lives on film. The elements that create context and connection will then quite naturally give rise to an artistic picture of karmic lawfulness, and enable the cinema to produce spiritually stimulating compositions in pictures and music. The enlivening of thinking experience that would need to be developed for this will manifest in an inner coherence of the picture-invoking imagination, thus in a content unachievable otherwise, however much money or high-tech know-how is employed.

In this way only the enlivening of thinking powers, the broadening of feelings and the consolidation of will impulses will open the gates through which spirit can enter cinematic experience. Where these gates remain shut, media consumers will continue to be offered unreal beings in human form, as well as demons, ghosts, monsters and aliens, rather than credible human beings. We can recall here that Steiner, in a lecture on 27 February 1917, urged the need for a counterweight to the addictive desire for sense reality which underpins film:[121] '…Just as we here develop an addictive descent below sensory perception, so at the same time we must ascend above sensory perception or in other words develop upward into the world of spirit…' Expression would be given to such striving in films that took up the theme of reincarnation and karma, both artistically and in accordance with reality.

The two most commonly used lures in ordinary narrative cinema are the speed with which action-packed events hurtle past the viewer (chases, collapsing cities, battles in which men or women in skin-tight clothes employ wearisomely unreal powers to gain the upper hand) or 'emotion cinema' with its many close-up shots and expressive minimalism. The latter exerts great fascination by using photogenic actors to entice a cinema audience to try to read the thoughts conveyed by their subtle, fleeting facial expressions. We might hope that this ability of actors to reflect inner states could be used increasingly for superordinate concerns, in other words in freer and more individual ways.[122] If so, cinema's naturalistic power of documentation would no longer be used solely for conveying occurrences of little psychological importance, which restrict cinematic enjoyment to mere recognition. After all, cinema-goers surely do not only seek a kind of awareness-dulling identification, but would also appreciate being challenged to raise themselves above their own subterranean and scarcely original egoisms.

It is clear from attempts so far made in cinema to engage with the theme of reincarnation and destiny, that we cannot expect those in positions of financial power in the visual entertainment industry to seek deeper that the usual psychological clichés. All such attempts have so far failed. The primary reason for this is that film producers themselves did not take the theme seriously, but took it up solely in order to meet a need for esoteric ideas that they had identified in the public. And most of their half-hearted efforts were also financial failures. Even undiscerning audiences, it seems, retain a residual ability to distinguish between mere pretence and narrative credibility and will not consume everything that is thrown at them.

And yet, given the relentless output of films each year, the film industry continually finds itself having to make new efforts to match its narratives with the now widespread assumption that 'there could be something in the theory of reincarnation'.[123] Thus the cinematic pot of narrative fantasies will continue to fill with scenarios of surprising complexity. The need to identify 'who is now who' will necessitate stereotypical conventions within this new genre of film. These will need to be smarter than the detective thriller made in England in which the murder victim of one life turned into the revenge-bent murderer of the next. This 90s black-and-white film solved the problem by having the same actor play both figures, distinguished only from each other by the moustache of the second.

We can run through such films at speed and they need not detain us: In *The Fountain* (2006), set between 1535 and 2500 AD, Tommy makes repeated efforts to cure Izzy from her fatal disease, finally managing it in a bubble of the space-time continuum; *Cloud Atlas* (2012) traces the lives of six linked individuals over several centuries. *The Mummy* (1999) and *The Mummy Returns* (2001) depict reincarnation only as some kind of horror scenario initiated

Rudolf Steiner 1907, photo, Fritz Hass

by evil, temple priests, with scorpions and desert landscapes. Finally *A Dog's Purpose* (2017) concerns the four lives of a dog with a gift for being reincarnated, and seems to be trying to 'prove' the fact of reincarnation at least to dog lovers — or in other words the majority of the viewing public — by showing how the dog in the last of his depicted lives meets his former and now elderly mistress, and is able to persuade her of the truth of reincarnation by replaying two tricks known only to the two of them. The film leaves unanswered the question of whether belief in reincarnating dogs can also be applied to human beings.[124] This whole mish-mash of films leads to one conclusion only: these filmmakers avoided any serious exploration of the subject of their films.

But we should also mention the genre of 'fake reincarnation films', which float in the same muddied waters. Some of these depict forms of possession of all kinds, and leave it unclear whether the person possessed and the possessing spirit are one and the same. Examples are *Crowley Back from Hell* (2008) and *Who Killed Marilyn* (2011). Then there are 'supposed reincarnation films' such as *Birth* (2004) in which a boy tries to persuade a woman (played by Nicole Kidman) that he is her reborn husband who was killed some years back. The film draws on the build-up of tension about the mystery at work here. Not until the end is it revealed that the precocious boy had seen the woman burying diaries containing details of her previous married life. Digging them up, he amazes the wife, with whom he is infatuated, with all kind of things she had only shared with her husband.

The difference between such films and 'genuine' reincarnation films is of little importance given that the latter also assume very shallow forms. *Made in Heaven* (1987), for instance, concerns itself with marriage engagements already concluded in heaven and with trying to ensure these are turned into proper marriages during earthly life. Much of this deals with efforts to discover who and where he or she is now.

If the individual human spirit fails in its earthly incarnation to develop understanding of itself as distinct from its body, this hinders all knowledge of reincarnation. A person will then lack the imprint of their essential identity within timeless spirit substance to which recall of a past life could relate. Knowledge of reincarnation that has been taking form in recent decades in the West is substantially different from ancient Indian techniques of liberation from the body. These were once practised to free the spirit from the cycle of rebirth, whereas the basis for individual knowledge of reincarnation has only arisen in our own times after an evolutionary path involving many embodiments.

If Rudolf Steiner had overseen filmmaking in his lifetime, he would naturally also have had to consider the specific techniques and technology of cinematic production, and here, as he did in the fields of dance, music, theatre, sculpture and architecture, he might well have pursued his own distinctive paths. In terms of today's techniques, he might perhaps have gone back to chemical picture creation in analogue technology, in which sunlight is directly involved in creating the picture. This was abandoned in favour of the Bayer matrix in digital photography, in which each shot is split into three colour values and subsequently recomposed (at the rate of at least 24 per second) as pixels by electrical impulses (in the case of professional camerawork, nowadays, several million pixels per image). This reversal would be roughly comparable to the current return of music lovers to the gramophone record. As mentioned before, improvements could be made in projection technique and the choice of screen so as to alleviate the anti-organic side-effects of picture production. That this has hardly ever been attempted is not due to technical or artistic considerations but only financial ones.[125]

Would this have resulted in a kind of 'niche anthroposophic' film? However one might imagine such an undertaking, production and marketing forms have changed completely since the early decades of cinema. The diversity of production and screening possibilities (as opposed to the possibilities of technical picture creation[126]) have grown hugely. From DVD discount shelves to video installations in high-end galleries, a wealth of culturally and economically varied forms of cinematic production and screening is now available.

Earlier I referred to the connection between a film specifically created for an open air festival, and related arts (theatre, dance, music). Here we need only shed the assumption that the quality of film art and its development is encompassed by the awards of Oscars, Palmes, Bears and Lions. At classic film festivals, too, it would be possible in future to make meaningful distinctions, though these would only emerge if there were real differences of approach and awareness in the creation of films.

A filmmaker such as Pasolini would surely have supported this. In an interview in 1970 he said:

> Shooting films for an elite is not a risk but a duty. Mass culture is the truly anti-democratic thing. An author or filmmaker is being democratic therefore if he refuses to serve mass culture and 'detaches' himself, working instead for people of real flesh and blood.[127]

Here too Tarkovsky had a different point of view. Although he accepted as inevitable the differentiations Pasolini made in respect of audiences, he could not welcome the fact. He wrote:

> A director's sense of time is naturally always an *assault* on the viewer. And in the same way, likewise, the inner world of the director is imposed on him. Now either the viewer 'falls into' your rhythm (into your world) and becomes your confederate, or he does not do so — which means that no communication comes about. Therefore there are also viewers who have an inner affinity with you, and others who are entirely alien to you. For me, this is not only completely natural but also unfortunately unavoidable.[128]

Rudolf Steiner would no doubt have considered the distinction between affinity and alienation to be unnecessary, since it does not affect the question of cinematic art and its deepening through a spiritually extended knowledge of the human being. He would have seen the art of film as one cultural means of expression among others for cultivating an urgently needed reunion of the human being with an intelligence enlarged through the collaboration of the cosmos. He gave voice to his motivation in this regard in his very last letter to the members of his Society. I cited this earlier, and will quote it once again now because of its fundamental importance:

> Our age needs knowledge that goes beyond nature since it must cope inwardly with the dangerous effects of a life that has sunk below the level of nature. Naturally we are not speaking here of returning to former cultural epochs, but of finding ways whereby human beings can create the right relationship both

with their cultural conditions and the cosmos. Nowadays very few people indeed feel the important spiritual tasks that are emerging for humankind. Electricity which, after its discovery, was praised as the very soul of natural existence, must be recognized as a force that can lead from nature down into sub-nature. But as human beings we must not slide down with it...

The 'dangerous effects' he speaks of, which impair our capacity of discernment, revealed themselves in Steiner's spiritual research as our subjection to the inspiration of ahrimanic spirits. These paralyse efforts to engender an image of the human being founded on inner self-enquiry, which seeks to grasp the configuring qualities of stages of reality that start from impulses initiated in high spiritual regions and progress through the worlds of soul and life (astral and etheric levels) down to materially consolidated tangibility. If the thought constraints and compulsions arising through the ahrimanic impetus were to come to unhindered expression, humanity would be transformed into a mentally controllable, digital system, in which the spiritual evolution of the earth would prematurely succumb to the sway of a self-enclosed, mechanistically governed cosmos.

In Steiner's aphoristic comments in *The Threshold of the Spiritual World* (Berlin, 1913), in the chapter 'On Recurring Lives on Earth and Karma', we find an account of the actions of unperceived ahrimanic intentions as spiritual clouding and darkening of human nature.[129] In relation to the previous quotation from Steiner, which refers to a sub-sensible or sub-natural level of reality, I have taken the liberty of transposing what he says in the next passage, about the relationship between 'spirit world' and 'sense world', to that between the 'natural sense world' and the 'virtual' world. In this case his words would read as follows:

One feels the virtual world to be a kind of mirror image of the natural sense world, but a mirror image in which the occurrences and beings of the natural sense world are not merely reflected but, despite being a mirror image, lead their own independent existence. It is as if a person were to see himself in a mirror and,

> as he saw himself, this mirror image were to take on a separate
> life. And thus we come to know spirit beings who bring about this
> independent life of the mirror image of the natural sense world...

The danger of 'ungood appearance', in which the living light of
true reality is at risk of suffocating, is something that scarcely
anyone today can overlook. We can meet this with our efforts to
emancipate our thinking, to expand our feeling and to consolidate
our will. Raising of the free will into full consciousness is the
distinguishing practice for contemporaries aware of the mission of
our era. It is predicated on a repeated willingness for renunciation
through the 'reining in' of thinking. A thinking, silently reined
in upon itself, contains the rhythmic counterpart to the thinking
will's devotion to the contents of pure concepts, within which
the spiritual context of the world manifests. This 'reining' creates
the organ for the universal life that pervades individual life.
In the inturned reflection of 'I think', the spiritual meaning of
'I live' forms itself into a bridge to the free, selfless will.

> This reining in of thinking gives rise to all true will development,
> which distinguishes the human being from the will-less activity
> of which animals are also capable. Only the consciousness first
> inwardly reined and then discharged again into activity, can be
> called will.[130]

But the opposite is also true. The power of internalized silence, of the
relinquishment of further thought contents, can only be strong to
the degree to which it has formed in the interlinking and overview
of 'abstract' concepts (that is, ones abstracted from sense qualities).
Only an ever renewed and rekindled motion in understanding of
inwardly determined conceptual patterning is able to transform
the subsequent erasing of all contents into spiritual seeing and
hearing within silent concentration. The freedom of will thus
initiated is the same at both poles of the fundamental rhythm of
human spiritual life.[131]

If we inwardly acknowledge and affirm this, we will not lose
our capacity of independent observation even within the virtual
world of the cinema. We will not apologise to John Huston and

his successors if we 'allow the terrible moment to arise when we attend again to ourselves',[132] and, by activating our freely governed observation, will be able to defend ourselves against all kinds of mass suggestion. 'Then film will not harm us however much we view cinematic images' (Rudolf Steiner).[133]

> Thus if our thinking view is the aspect of our being that is never lost and always inviolable, nevertheless it is not available to us without our efforts. It has to be always activated anew. While it is true that, in waking life, we can never entirely dispense with this activity, we can however forget it by failing to make it into its own object. In doing so we deny the will aspect of our being, which otherwise belongs to the subconscious, precisely at the place where we can raise it into awareness. This will awareness is the distinguishing characteristic of the modern human being. Yet he himself must decide whether he wishes to develop this conscious awareness or not.[134]

Epilogue (fictional)

In 1866, on his way from Berlin, Joseph Vogelsang crossed over the border into the kingdom of Bavaria. A cattle-dealer who was heading home from a market town in Thuringia with an empty wagon had taken him and his St Verena peep-box this far. Since he had no Bavarian money, this marked the end of his vehicular transport. Vogelsang now had to walk on foot, pulling his box behind him, wrapped in woollen covers and safely strapped together. In the first town in Bavaria that he came to, where he would look for accommodation for the night, he hoped to find the best way of continuing his journey.

He was exhausted and downcast. His 'microplastic depictions' were no longer of interest to anyone. The few coins he had earned on his last trip were far from sufficient to meet the costs of his present journey. Children who had taken a peep into the box even asked for their money back, saying that 'there was nothing moving' inside. Evidently, they had already taken a look at more up-to-date and fashionable boxes, in which horses and athletes performed endless, circling movements. People simply had no idea how much effort had gone into the making of his model. Should he perhaps introduce a small, hidden pipe to make water flow through the brook, which the pious hermit called the 'little Jordan'? That at least would bring some movement into his miniature world. As he thought about this, he was sitting not far from the road in the shadow of an apple tree, leaning against the box that he had now put down on the ground. The sun was hot, and sleep overcame him.

Vogelsang dreamed that he was in Jerusalem, and that it looked just as it did in his box. He himself appeared to be one of the many birds that he had modelled by hand and placed on the tree beside the brook. Thunderclouds were threatening, and so he sought refuge in the Church of the Cross. Here people were sitting on benches as if turned to stone and all staring at an empty, whitewashed wall. He heard the dark voice of the hermit, murmuring an equally dark poem as the storm raged outside:

> I heard a marvel from the giant worm,
> From the snake that swallowed up whole worlds.
> Spiralling round in a hundred coils
> It had wound itself ready for heavy sleep.
>
> The smooth body, the jellied eel of itself
> Is formed of a thousand scales,
> And shining through its pale mesentery is seen
> The masticated bilge of chewed-up worlds.
>
> Streets and cities, towers and gateways,
> The bags and baggage of busy life,
> Laughter and tears, all that once lived
> Now passes endlessly through the queue of its gut.
>
> The fleeting life of ongoing growth
> Now magically lifted out of time,
> The frozen drops of the living stream
> The lindworm guards till daylight breaks.
>
> Then he rears up and unwinds his length.
> He gags on the pellets, spews out the gobbets.
> In scathing appearance the ruins arise:
> They live — they hover — through space and through time.[135]

The storm faded and the sun broke through the clouds. People streaming out of the church gathered round his box as if they were expecting a grand spectacle. He undid the leather straps and took off the coverings. And now something miraculous occurred: the walls of the box became transparent and began to move. The box grew until Vogelsang and all the others watching were encompassed within it. No one needed the peepholes any longer, which were now situated far behind them. The scenery of the St Verena hermitage had vanished. At each side hung numerous lamps which slowly went out after a while. In keen expectation, the people saw how a heavy red velvet curtain divided and revealed a further space that gradually began to breathe in light and shadow, its images hinting at the scenes of their daily world which had now been swallowed up by the darkness that engulfed their bodies and had been sucked up into wholesome oblivion by the brightness of their hearts. From the peepholes behind them a voice called out into the auditorium:

> Pictures rise up, cast on the water!
> Intuit dreams, connect intimations!
> Reveal the mystery, oh mirror substantial,
> The eye has perceived it, imbued with its gleam.
>
> Experience now vision, cleansed by the will.
> Recognize love, that configured the image.
> A song lifts, arises, a poem in light,
> A meaningful story the ether creates.
>
> Towers and mountains, forests and streets,
> Now moving, now slowing congregation of peoples.
> Secret glances, significant steps and all forms:
> Brought hither, it seems, like the body of the beloved.
>
> Etched by the sun's rays in sensitive substance,
> A creation is born with interpretative intent.
> Hymns rise to the now resurrected experience
> Of eyes that were blind and sense-drunk on their food.
>
> And deep in their hearts, the pondering ones know this:
> Sacred the will that commands their perceptions.
> Sacred their succession, in time's growth well-ordered.
> Sacred their karma, the true fount of poetry!
>
> How is it, I asked you, that singing you pour out
> A potion of images from a star-bright jug,
> So that an etheric rose fragrance surrounds
> The Redeemer who sustains us through infinite time?

Appendix 1:
Epistemological Foundations and the four levels of reality

In the *festschrift* celebrating 20 years of the Solothurn Film Days, Swiss cinema's most important film festival, I wrote the following:

> Understanding interconnections is the fundamental practice from which all others should emerge if one is not to relinquish all spirit in the throes of planning and scheduling activity. One of the primary questions that has to be asked in relation to modern visual media is this: Can the filmmaker retain his voice, his expressive faculty, in relation to his material, the film exposure itself? The search for the linguistic structure of cinema has ended with no outcome for all who have so far undertaken this quest (Metz, Pasolini, Eco, Barthes etc.).
>
> This is (without embarking here on insights derived from inner observation) connected with the difficulty of initiating within the visual media the aesthetic equilibrium, the dialectical process, between expression and impression... As a result of the mechanization of depictive naturalism, film material is consonantally remodelled to such a degree that it severely impairs any form of participation that both leaves viewers free and liberates them. On the other hand, the cinematic stuttering that breathlessly states what is depicted to be 'thus and thus and thus and thus...' leads to the perversion of the human capacity for experience. With the narrative convention that has hardened as a result of the film business's expectations, the 'hypnotic monster' (Pasolini) that a film always is, is merely veiled in the scanty outfit of the arbitrary. What is expected of a 'good (i.e. successful) film', is the abasement of the viewer to become a consumer of states of self-forgetting...[136]

We must also consider the fact that, in Rudolf Steiner's spoken comments — he did not write anything specifically about the medium of film — he was addressing listeners familiar with the bases and terms of his spiritual science. Without taking this into account, his characterization of the medium of film, which runs counter to the cultural assumptions of the world at large, would all too easily be exposed to misunderstandings and unjustified reproach. In what follows, therefore, I will need to summarize Steiner's idea of reality as outcome of an inwardly observed counter-stream of spiritual-ideational shaping forces, and of concepts whereby sense perceptions are formatively imbued and ordered, in order to position Steiner's assessment of the unreality of film naturalism. In cognitive penetration, it falls to sense perception to represent sense-free ideas in their sensory individualization. Thus reality is the outcome of a balance consciously established in cognition in the reciprocal interaction of substance and form (of what is passively and actively given).

Ordinary, everyday consciousness feels the world that presents itself to the senses to be a given because it is inevitably asleep to its own spiritual participation in the process of rendering objects and movements conscious. This can lead to the assumption that reality, even if it represents itself in nothing but sensory, subjective ideas, is still present without a thinking subject. A study of existence (ontology) which draws on inner observation to clarify the participation of conceptual formative forces, forms the basis for penetrating the dynamic of reality formation and reality loss and, connected with this, an experientially based distinction between reality and illusion.[137] This is also the premise for any media science and 'media education' that is worthy of the name.

Awakening to our own participation in the emergence of world creation and world processes means to the same degree to awaken to our own I nature, the latter implicit in every awakening. Those who object that our participation in the process of reality can relate only to the contents of our subjective consciousness and not to an 'objective world', about which we can know nothing 'for certain', take flight from observation of the pertinent factors by resorting to the customary dream of a world that transcends consciousness.

The reality of the I does not consist in the worn-out memory coinage of the sensory contents of consciousness. Its content, supplied by intuition, is distinct from the spirit-blind 'I feeling' of someone who, involved in sense perception, hopes to find in its unreliable present a firm reality, and to invoke what is only momentary in Faust's words of 'Oh tarry, do, so lovely as you are!'[138] The real I arises as fruit of deep-delving self-knowledge, which awakens to the reality of world of spirit as the origin, hidden within the ordinary mind, of concepts and ideas, of feelings and impulses of will. Perception of the true I liberates a self-awareness incarcerated in the subjective dungeon of seemingly insuperable division between I and world, that seeks to nourish itself solely from the dissociative power of its alienation from the spirit.

I have included amongst Steiner's few comments on the cinema in this volume, a remark that is decisive in this context, that he made in a conversation that was not made public until April 1983. This remark triggered an 'internal anthroposophic' debate about its credibility — a debate that I examined earlier. Apart from this there exists to my knowledge only a single written comment in which Steiner (albeit only implicitly) referred to the problem of technical entertainment or artistic media.[139] As we have seen, this comment, examined earlier, contains a legacy of importance for the future: his last written remark altogether, which was published only two weeks after his death — on 30 March 1925 — in the journal for which it was intended.[140]

The following aspects — even if we can scarcely ever account for them — can be distinguished in our usual thoughts and ideas, as we form these within our social milieu and in the context of our naturally given surroundings (I am leaving aside the visual media, for now, which give rise to a significant modification of thinking consciousness):

4) Let us start by enumerating, as it were, from below upward, and from sensory externality, advancing inward from there into soul observation. Initially it is the localized, solid forms of physical-mineral nature and the objects or artefacts made by human beings which, the moment we turn our attention to them through a corresponding sense organ, allow an external sense impression to live on in us as thought or mental picture. But the sense organs themselves do not perceive. In sleep the ear is just as functionally capable as in waking life. Fixing my gaze in a particular direction my attention can wander at will within the field of vision, so that the focus of attention alone will allow new details to become perceptible, for instance things in the corner of my eye. It would be unnecessary to point out that it is human beings who perceive by directing their attention and thus invoking the function of their sense organs if it were not for the widespread, erroneous idea that sense organs compel sense reality to shift into consciousness.

Secondly, we can consider the outer stimulus to thinking arising in the form of impressions left in us from lifeless things or plants that are merely outwardly set in motion, or self-moving animal and human bodies with their more or less expressive movements. No less than unmoving objects at rest, movements only come to our awareness with our thinking participation, although the latter usually unfolds unconsciously and, within the medial sensory environment, as we will see, is physiologically dulled. To understand this it is useful to leave behind the idea of thinking as word recall. The power of thinking is intrinsically more closely connected with pure memory than with word pictures, as can be recognized through becoming aware of outer movement processes.

A movement is a gliding sequence of movement stages manifested by a self-moving body, say a bird in flight, or becoming apparent through the outer influence of forces as in the motion of ocean waves. Here the eye perceives time-limited movement cross-sections (the movement stages) rather than their connection to an overall movement. The latter is predicated on memory and thus the capacity to connect present with past. Memory as a capacity fundamental to biographical development is not sensory in nature but mental/ spiritual. The self-aware human being must and can only develop it in free inner activity. By contrast, obsessive thoughts do not arise as an act of recall but arise in and due to psychological passivity.[141]

3) Then we must consider the images which, after contact with sense perception, pass over into our awareness, and which we distinguish from primary sense experiences by virtue of the fact that we can re-enliven them in memory, whereas sensory pictures themselves are tied to spatial-temporal coincidence with our sense organs. Here memory does not in some way conjure up sense impressions again out of the memory's cache but leads to a new ideation of the pictures that arose during primary contact with our subconscious participation. This remark is necessary due to the widespread error that sees the memory as a brain-localized storage space, and memory as a largely passive download operation. This preconception arises by overlooking inner, soul participation both in primary sense picturing and memory.

2) At this level of self-reflection, we grasp concepts and ideas, by means of which we bring sensory experiences — whether these are primary or mediated in the form of memory — into a connection that satisfies our faculty of cognition. Either we experience the content of the concepts and ideas intuitively in self-aware, free thinking activity, or we adopt this in a form mediated by others as word-bound and prejudged thinking.

The following must be said here: general concepts (ideas) as connection-forming and shaping forces must, as we already saw, be sharply distinguished from words and the thoughts that either cause them or come to be associated with them. Even if the linguistic configuration of intuitively grasped concepts and ideas is necessary in certain instances in order for us to consolidate awareness of them and to render us capable of outward communication, their objective, spiritual content arises neither through individual activation of thinking nor through its 'translation' into an available form of language, but is found by inner observation to be independent of these. The concept of the circle that can concretize my understanding of the horizon on the open sea, exists independently of my thinking it, and is not identical with the words 'circle', 'cerchio' or 'kpyr', with which various languages refer to it. Independent examination of the following statement by Rudolf Steiner in his *The Philosophy of Freedom* is a prerequisite for observing the reciprocal interpenetration of the formative forces inherent in ideas and the sensory content of perception: 'Concepts and ideas arise through thinking. What a concept is cannot be said with words. Words can only draw a person's attention to the fact that he possesses concepts.'[142]

1) Finally, let us place the nature of the I itself into the field of inwardly observed experience. In the I is rooted the concept-forming activity which works back formatively in turn upon the I itself. Primary reflection between I consciousness and thinking activity cannot be elaborated here in the detail required by its importance. But a few indications may be helpful for assuring oneself, through inner observation, that I formation as an archetypal rhythm of self-reflection is not merely a subjective process. Merely subjective thoughts drawn from memory must, rather, fall silent where the 'I' takes responsibility for I cognition. The following sentences from Steiner's freedom philosophy (1894) pointed to this fact over a century ago:

> The activity a person exercises as thinking being is thus not merely subjective but one that is neither subjective nor objective, surpassing these two concepts. I must never say that my individual subjectivity thinks, but this subjectivity itself lives, rather, by the grace of thinking. Thinking is therefore an element that leads me beyond my self and connects me with objects. But it also separates me from them at the same time by confronting me as subject with them.[143]

Pointers to the process of I formation and the hindrances to it:

Each morning when I open my eyes and perceive my surroundings, I know, founded on my subconscious memory, that the ceiling, the bed and the wall belong to my room. Is the immediate knowledge that it is I who is remembering this likewise founded on the sum of memories of all I concepts formed previously in my waking life? By no means! Unlike with sensory ideas, we do not rely on previous I conceptions to gain a content for our present one. The experience of I consciousness is an inner will process that starts in the depths of the 'I' and is reflected in our conceptual idea of the I. The mirroring function belongs here to the brain and neural activity. The content of the original, primary I being is reflected in the distinct — and as far as its originating content is concerned, unillumined — I thought, from which it must be distinguished.[144] The sense of I connected with the thought or conception of the I is available to daily consciousness, without outer cause, in every waking moment. Thus the I conception distinguishes itself from all other thoughts such as this blanket, this bed or this wall, which can only be formed where a corresponding act of perception exists.

Ordinary perception and thinking do not unfold in their essential nature but consist of a conditioned reactivation of subconscious factors. This is significant in this account, since the cinema experience is sought by many in the hope that the recognitional patina of personal life experience will be re-enlivened with a 'new' freshness of the senses, or in other words one mediated by something as yet unknown.

Everyone can get a clear idea of these processes when observing children's speech and thinking development. Their imaginative play serves to test their tentative expressions of soul, which they articulate in provisionally (playfully) created, inwardly sculpted sound patterns, seeking to interpret and shape their sense experiences. It is in this way that we all learned to orientate ourselves in the sense world and to establish ourselves in self-awareness within it.

We find our access to perception of what is ordinarily unobserved in particular objects or occurrences through voluntary acts of observation that must be repeatedly conducted. In doing so we need to answer this question precisely: *What am I perceiving — for instance in a corkscrew, a feeling of happiness or a bank of cloud, and what ideational, conceptual element am I complementing it with?* And also:

What have I already added to this so that an object can appear to me as an outwardly coherent whole? Without a meditative practice focused on these things, we scarcely become aware of the purely perceptual element. Exceptions to this are, say, dream-tinged moments when we wake up in strange surroundings, or a drug-induced state of consciousness that makes daily awareness fall apart into its 'inner' and 'outer' components, at the same time obstructing free observation of them. Likewise, in rare moments of terror in a life-threatening situation, in which we become aware of the purely perceptual element as an entirely non-qualitative singularity on the one hand, and on the other of our self as the entity that seeks understanding, we experience the archetypal polarities of substance and form, of light and darkness, from whose unity and interpenetration daily reality emerges.

Appendix 2:
Account of a proposed film,
with screenplay synopsis

Reto Andrea Savoldelli
Teufenberg, CH-9107 Urnäsch, Switzerland   31 March 1973

Screenplay application
(To the grant committee of the Swiss Film Commission and the Pro
Helvetia Foundation)

1. General thoughts on film (extract)

Most films made in recent years are profoundly inhuman. While
questions about the meaning of film for human beings and the intrinsic
nature of the cinematic experience still figured in the early history of
cinema, in general film production has pushed such questions ever
further into the background. Technical possibilities have been used
without reflection, and the standard of quality is held to be the power
of film as spectacle, its sensory effect on the mass of viewers...

Countering this materialistic cultural stance, which has taken
almost exclusive hold on the cinematic means of production, a
current will now gradually emerge within the history of cinema
that focuses on ensouling film as opposed to rendering it demonic
(through coldly calculating, impersonal and power-seeking technology). The film camera and the microphone will come into the
hands of people who are moved by heartfelt moral impulses, and
who love film for its as yet scarcely tapped capacities to depict
inner realities. Technical aids will lose their coldness, camera and
microphone will become extensions of our sense organs, screen
images will render visible the living soul in its primary activities,

and image sequences, montage, will reveal a pattern woven from spiritual imaginations, that bear the stamp of an artist (not of a computer), whose organic logic will resemble that of a rose or a lion.

2. Account of the project, 'You don't step twice in the same river or After me will come the one who was before me.'

Work on my films has so far always progressed as follows: first I shoot a short sequence of images, fleeting thoughts, semi-conscious ones, distinguished from other products of the imagination by their filmic potential. Sometimes they are triggered by a sense impression or an experience, though usually they arise without an outer cause. Before deciding on a new film, I cultivate this inner, filmic engendering of images and tone while my conscious participation in the material increases; and at a somewhat more advanced stage of work, I start to write things down, so that energetic thought work can trace and elaborate the context of the stream of imagination. However, this is by no means an arbitrary act but is often connected with the feeling of recreating the unity in these ideas which they already possessed before I became conscious of them.

What is so far clear about my forthcoming film, which I have provisionally called 'You don't step twice in the same river (Heraclitus) or After me will come the one who was before me (John, 1.15)', is the following: It will centre on the life of an individual as considered in terms of karma; that is, in two sequences the film will trace two successive incarnations of the same person. Accordingly, it will be divided into two parts entitled respectively, 'The Crusade' and 'The Cross'. This structural polarity appears very fruitful both in terms of thought and form. Through an account of the relationships of these two incarnations, an attempt will be made to depict a spiralling development around a centre, whose lawfulness sustains both the single individual and the whole of humanity. Illumination of the laws of evolution that determine the whole human organism will supply social and historical aspects so greatly absent — due to a failure of understanding — in my previous films.

THE CRUSADE (Part 1)

Part 1 is set during seven years at the beginning of the thirteenth century. After a brief prelude on a theatre stage in which, as previously in *Stella da Falla*, a humorous foregrounding of the nature of media seeks to help the viewer enter more easily and consciously into the film itself, we see, to begin with, the daily life of our chief protagonist in the small castle in the mountains, the seat of his progenitors, somewhere in Germany or possibly in Burgenland (Austria). Here he lives in close proximity with his father, mother and numerous sisters as a young, newly married lord.

The family, bequeathed a small estate after generations of faithful service, is paralysed by long years of political and religious tension characteristic of that era: the increase in power of Popes (the rise of papal legates to the detriment of power previously exercised by bishops), the disputes between the Staufer Emperor and Rome, crusade fever, the founding of knights' orders (the Johannites, the Templars, German orders), the emergence of 'heresies', above all in southern France and Italy, which turn against the increasing worldliness of the Roman Curia, the persecution of heretics, the Jewish pogroms etc. The work the family has dutifully done over generations now receives no acknowledgement. Their lord of the manor is also usually abroad (taking part in Italian campaigns by the Staufers, and in crusades). Thus, increasingly in enforced isolation, the family witnesses the tumult of the times that is also apparent in surrounding villages.

Our chief protagonist feels ever more strongly that his task is to seek some remedy for this spiritual lethargy in his parental home. He first thinks that their isolation from the scene of world events is causing this apathy. One morning, therefore, he rides south together with his friend, a young farmer, who lives in a homestead directly below the castle, and with whom he has grown up in close proximity. In conversations with his friend and in numerous meetings with wayfaring traders, journeying knights, farmers who have fallen on hard times, thieves, minstrels, beggar monks and poets, he gradually gains understanding of the prevailing circumstances, but not of the real reasons for all the tumult and suffering. The melancholy that has driven him from home grows into an aimless longing. He keeps directing these yearnings at ever new objectives. For a while, the two think that their duty is to take part in the crusades proclaimed by the Popes. They travel to southern France and take ship at Marseille. Since the excommunicated Kaiser Frederick II keeps postponing the long-due Fifth Crusade (1228/1229), in southern France the two friends have a long period of waiting during which they come into contact with the continually spreading 'heretical Christian' culture of Provence, founded primarily on the Cathar sect. Through the troubadours who have emerged from this cultural milieu the two become acquainted with the Grail poems which, at this particular period, are having a renewing effect on the peoples of Provence. The chief protagonist projects his blind longing upon the imaginative content of the Grail story, and through this Christianization of his desires feels greatly enlivened.

The friends then experience the threatening approach of the crusading army under Simon de Montfort, Earl of Leicester, whom Innocence III has mobilized against the movement of the 'heretics', who are beginning to have an influence also on the worldly powers in southern France. The chief protagonist must simply await his fate, like the mouse waiting for the snake to strike. In a mass pyre, he dies by fire with other 'heretics' who have been driven together. To the very last moment he stays true to his longing for a just humanity sustained by love — a spiritual strength that is still to bear fruit.

Shortly before his arrest he had separated from his friend, who now rides northwards, heading back home. At the castle, in the meantime, the chief protagonist's parents and two sisters have died. His wife has foreseen the news of his death.

THE CROSS (Part 2) and the connections between
Part 1 and Part 2

In the second part of the film, entitled 'The Cross', we find the same individual again, now in a small town in Switzerland in the twentieth century. However, in Part 2 the chief protagonist will never be visible (except possibly for a fraction of a second as he passes a mirror). Camera and microphone will replace him. Whereas in Part 1 the viewer could look upon the workings of destiny as if from without, in Part 2 he sees things from an extremely subjective perspective. The soul characteristics of the chief protagonist as apparent in Part 1 are something the viewer must now engender within himself again in Part 2. Thus he will rediscover many things from Part 1 again as if in inverted form.

In schematic terms, the two perspectives could be registered like this:[145]

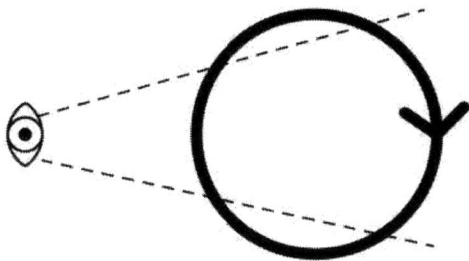

Part 1
Viewer

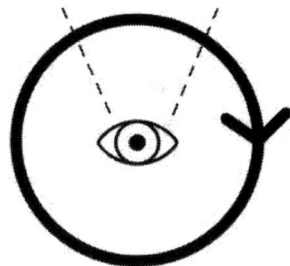

Part 2
Running film

In Part 2, the viewer experiences the chief protagonist's inner life, in an encounter with the following outer events during the seven days that comprise Part 2 (Monday morning to Sunday night): He wakes up in a small, rented room (he is unmarried), takes the morning tram to his job as a shift worker in a factory (e.g. a paper factory), passes through crowds of people at the station, at the entrance to a football stadium, at a political rally; then in the evening takes the tram home again and watches TV in the living room of the family where he is a lodger. On Friday evening he goes to the cinema, and on Sunday he goes for a walk with the family of a colleague from work.

These mundane outer occurrences are rendered coherent by the person's rich inner life, and interpreted through it: an inner monologue, sequences of thought, memory images, just the hint of a higher recall breaking through in antipathies and sympathies originating from the past life. Thus, for instance, he is deeply stirred by the sight of an open fire that he must force himself to look at. These inner realities interpenetrate the outward images. I will attempt to directly incorporate in the film medium, without symbolic translation, the inner realism in which, in the daily life of every person, external impressions are combined with thoughts and ideas rising up from within.

My conception here is that the cinematic experience will not, as it usually is, be determined by the production method, the style of montage or the outward standpoint adopted by the director in his staging, but that selection of the images and auditory impressions will be felt to originate, in Part 2, with the invisible protagonist. In other words, the camera lens and microphone are enlivened and intensified to become sense organs and what falls upon these technical eyes and ears appears, in turn, as determined by an underlying subjectivity. This inner life will be experienced as a real and living receiver by virtue of the fact that it momentarily assimilates the images and auditory effects.

By this mode of depiction, key differences between nowadays and circumstances in the thirteenth century will become apparent, for instance, regarding the causes of actions by the chief protagonist in Part 1 as opposed to Part 2. In the latter, insight into cultural and spiritual contexts will emerge that can go as far as to be consciously grasped in the mind of the protagonist. In Part 1, by contrast, we see a blind devotion to a longing that is embraced as true and that becomes the basis for outer deeds. Developments that cannot mature fully in Part 1 find their swift continuation in Part 2 and initially leave the chief protagonist as if hanging in the air, something that comes to expression also in his outward circumstances. This lasts until the moment when he recognizes his almost terrifying freedom and, with inner awareness, begins to shape his own thinking, feelings and actions.

Differences between the two parts, and the process of evolution that intervenes between them, can be exemplified more precisely in the following two titles and the subsequent scenes, which are intended to convey a polar meditative significance:

CRUSADE

Movement. Longing.
Restlessness. Bowstring (arrow
and bow). The journey to the
Cross. The misapprehended
journey to the 'sacred
Jerusalem' which is not the 'new
Jerusalem' of the Apocalypse
(the failure of then historical
crusades!). The form of the
Romanesque Church with its
focus on the front altar. Feeling.
Unconsciousness.

A scene from Part 1

*We see the chief protagonist on
a winter's evening, at twilight,
running from his castle into the
open to escape the burdensome
atmosphere in the castle. He cries
and shouts aloud, falls to his knees
in the deep snow and walks on.
He is dressed only in light clothes
but is equipped with bow and
quiver. As he carries on walking,
he puts an arrow to the bow and
shoots at random, high into the
cloudy sky. Though nothing but
the wind can be heard, blood falls
upon the snow in front of him.
He kneels to look at it, resting
on his bow. The connection
between his explosion of
feelings and the suffering of
a creature remains unclear.
As he remains in this stance,*

CROSS

The events at Golgotha in
Jerusalem as the nodal point
of world-creating powers.
The nodal point. Centredness.
Tranquillity. The form of
the human figure. Decision.
The central form of the Grail
chapel. The octagonal 'Castel
del Monte' of Frederick II.
Thinking. Consciousness.

A scene from Part 2

The chief protagonist has got up
very early in the morning and,
before he starts work, is walking
along the banks of a river. In the
morning sun, which is already
gaining brilliance, he suddenly
sees a few fishermen who stand
motionless with their rods.
A fish has bitten. The fisherman
reels in the line, snatches the
fish from the hook and throws
the flapping, white-scaled fish
carelessly over his shoulder
onto the black tarmac of the
road.

In a close-up of the
quivering white fish on the
black tarmac, the protagonist is
suddenly moved — by direct
and conscious understanding
— to intervene meaningfully:

the camera rises from a worm's-eye view to one hundred/two hundred metres above his bowed back into the sky (helicopter). Once the earth can scarcely be seen any more, a flock of wild geese come winging past.

he picks up the fish and throws it in a high curve back into its element. He comes to join the fisherman, who shakes his head in mute acquiescence and goes on staring into the flowing river.

Notes and references

1. This can be seen today in Solothurn's Blumenstein Museum, ten minutes walk from the Verena Gorge. See the pictures at the end of the book. Photos © Museum Blumenstein.
2. See the plate section. And see www.HieronymusFilm.ch for the cinematic works of R.A. Savoldelli.
3. Whereas Anglo-Americans think of films in terms of 'shooting', Germans speak of 'turning' a film in reference to the original hand-cranking device, even though film reels have been driven by electric motor since the 1920s.
4. The chief protagonist in the novel by film-maker Hieronymus Halbeisen, 'Hieronymus — On Cinema and Love in Eras of Reincarnation', takes up this invention (and others as well) in the overall context of the humanization of film techniques. There he describes further technical details — see www.das-seminar.ch (German language website).
5. They include 'Zur mediumistischen Nature des Kinos', in *Korrespondenz — Zeitschrift für freie Jugendarbeit und Sozialorganik*, July 1983; 'Nur das Persönliche ist das Allgemeine' in *The show must go on...* a festschrift celebrating 20 years of the Solothurn Film Days, 1966–1985 (edited by Ivo Kummer/Heinz Urben); a piece on the mirroring problem in general, 'Der Vorzeit Wissen' in *Zeitschrift für freie Jugendarbeit und Sozialorganik*, November 1985; *Was hat Kino mit Reinkarnation zu tun*, SeminarVerlag 2013; *Vom Drehbuch zum Roman*, SeminarVerlag 2013 and *Die Erwärmung des Spiegels*, lecture in Dornach on 7 April 2018, SeminarVerlag. Excerpts from this, likewise under the title of 'Die Erwärmung des Spiegels', are also found in notes by Hieronymus Halbeisen in the Hieronymus novel.
6. Primarily established by John Watson (1913), who attacked 'introspection' and also psychoanalysis as being 'unscientific', and who saw the human being as a 'black box' that could only be explored and understood through a scientifically 'objective' methodology. This, he said, required every behaviour to be analysed in terms of stimulus/

response. He was followed by B.F. Skinner in the books *Science and Human Behavior* (1953) and *Beyond Freedom and Dignity* (1971).

7. Quoted from *Wie sie filmen*, Gütersloh, 1966, p. 223.

8. 'Directors' who dedicate themselves without further distraction to this 'cinematic subject' have in the meantime become the industry's big earners. The amateur porn industry has likewise established itself at a subordinate 'artistic level'. The documentary devoted to it, 'Hot Girls Wanted' (premiered at the Sundance Film Festival 2015) noted in passing that download rates for its products are higher than, say, for the film platform Netflix (which produced the documentary), Twitter and Amazon put together.

9. Authors of this school included Cohen-Séat, E. Souriteau, Roland Barthes, Cristian Metz, André Bazin, Merlon-Ponty, J.F. Lyotard, and latterly Gilles Deleuze.

10. Rudolf Steiner spent seven years in Weimar working as the first editor of Goethe's scientific writings.

11. R. Steiner, in answers to questions after his lecture on 5 January 1922 in Dornach. This was the fourteenth of a total of sixteen lectures to teachers, entitled 'The Healthy Development of the Physical Body as Basis for the Free Unfolding of the Soul and Spirit.'

12. Bibliography: H. Lehmann, *Die Kinematographie*, 1911; Konrad Lange, *Das Kino in Gegenwart und Zukunft*, 1920; Béla Balázs, *Visible Man or the Culture of Film*, 1924; Rudolf Harms, *Die Philosophie des Films*, 1926; Heinz Richter, *Filmgegner von heute — Filmfreude von morgen*, 1919; Rudolf Arnheim, *Film als Kunst*, 1932; Siegfried Kracauer, *Theory of Film* (subtitled *The Redemption of Physical Reality*), 1960.

13. *Claude Monet*, Fondation Beyeler, 22 January to 28 May 2017.

14. R.Steiner, *Leading Thoughts* (1925), no. 35.

15. See, for instance, the interview 'Sergiu Celibidache on his philosophy of music', youtube.com

16. R.A.Savoldelli, Third video sura from the West-East Video Lounge. https://vimeo.com/channels/hieronymusvideolounge/page:2

17. In the journal *Info3*, Frankfurt a.M., 1983.

18. 'Ahriman, spiritual being, the power of darkness in the Persian religion of Zarathustra, who opposes the power of light, the Sun God Ahura Mazdao (great wisdom). In general an entity who strongly develops the capacity of intellectual reason and, in the natural and human context, embodies the principle of hardening, leading also

to materialization and mechanization of life processes. The polar counter-force to this is the principle of fantastical illusion and seductive temptation embodied in Lucifer.' (Wolfgang Veit, *Bewegte Bilder*, Stuttgart 1993, p. 149). The attainment of equilibrium in the individual soul between these two powers that oppose the human being's free development (and not, say, the eradication of their influences!) is the core task of the human being. It is clear that both figures participate in the overall phenomenon of our technical advances, and thus also in the cinema too: Ahriman through his fundamental cultivation of technology, and Lucifer through the objectification of narrative dream-world content, thus concealing the central human task described.

19. Prior to this Steiner had described the negative effect of induction current in the context of increasing electrification (nowadays we would call it electrosmog), citing the two representative examples of telegraphy and film. Elsewhere he mentioned the huge increases in the speed of news dissemination that would come in future, connected with a growing vacuity and difficulty of understanding such rapid news bombardment.

20. In numerous lectures, and in the chapter 'Some Effects of Initiation' in his book, *Knowledge of the Higher Worlds*, Rudolf Steiner described how feelings, thoughts and intentions manifest in higher worlds mantled in the forms of true imaginations. The Cypriot esotericist, Attheshlis, the 'Magus of Strovolos' (the title of the first of several books about him by Kryiacos Markides, published by Knauer) uses the term 'elemental' for these, and has described them very aptly.

21. In its issue on 7 October 2017. This influential weekly was founded in 1905, and is sold in 84 countries.

22. Harvey Weinstein, founder of the Miramax Film Production Company, which was sold to Walt Disney Studios. Its films and the actors in them, have won around a hundred Oscars.

23. For example, a single gameshow, Dota-2, which took place in August 2017 in Seattle and handed out 24 million dollars in prizemoney, had an auditorium audience of 17,000 people and was followed live all over the world by millions of people on big screens and via Twitch.tv. The winner was a Berliner, 24-year-old KuroKy, who, with his team was able to take home around 11 million dollars.

24. Thus H. Weinstein, too, has gone to Europe now to have 'sex-withdrawal therapy'. [He has since been sentenced to 23 years in Prison—Ed.]

25. See for instance the German-American film *Cinemania* from 2002, which documents the life of five film addicts in New York.

26. Early instances of what is meant by this, albeit very imperfect ones, can be found in my films *Lydia* (1968) and *Stella da Falla* (1971). In the latter the initially chronological account, starting with the seventeenth birthday of the chief protagonist in her former life in the medieval period, is gradually superseded by an initiation event.

27. A term used by the film producer and screenplay author Wolf Otto Pfeiffer in Berlin, which lent its name to the 'Association to Further the Spirit in Film'.

28. Cf. Steiner's comment in Berlin on 27 February 1917, p. 22.

29. This was patented a century ago by Grosse in Berlin (see Rudolf Harms, *Die Philosophie des Films*). A development of this is being used again today for vacuous tourist attractions in the form of spatializing water vapour. An example of this is the show 'Wings of Time' on the island of Sentosa, Singapore.

30. As demonstrated in the film *The Artist* (2011) by Michel Hazanavicuis, a stimulating personal reflection on film history. He dispensed entirely with tonal language, which did not diminish his success but underpinned it. Here, exceptionally, producers were willing to take a risk with a film that offered the viewer no known terrain.

31. P.P. Pasolini, *Reihe Hanser* no. 232, p. 57.

32. P.P. Pasolini, ibid., p. 99.

33. Zeylmans was a priest of The Christian Community, a movement for religious renewal supported and overseen by Steiner.

34. R. Steiner, lecture in Penmaenmawr on 29 August 1923.

35. Among other things, he described how cattle would 'go mad' if — something entirely unknown back then — they were fed with animal-based fodder. The BSE disease in cattle, caused by animal additives to cattle feed, was generally referred to in the 90s as 'mad cow disease'.

36. See extracts from the proposal in the appendix.

37. The lecture, held in Arlesheim (Switzerland), was published (without the ensuing discussion) in July 1983 in *Korrespondenz des Seminars für Freie Jugendarbeit, Kunst und Sozialorganik*.

38. The film project was studied and rejected by the following producers and foundations among others: SRF Zurich (Martin Schmassmann and Christine Dobler), X-Films Berlin, Arthur Cohn Basel, Triluna-Film Zurich, Vega Film Zurich, Cara Film Bern, Rommel Film Berlin,

Maximage Zurich, Fama Film Zurich, T+C Hoehn Film Zurich, Presence Production Zurich (N. Burger and S. Häberling), Richterich Stiftung CH-Laufen, Nestlé Foundation Lausanne, Software Stiftung Darmstadt (a foundation with strong links to anthroposophy, today the funder and administrator of Alanus University for Art and Society in Alfter, Germany).

39. R.A.Savoldelli, *Hieronymus — über Kino in Zeiten der Reinkarnation*, SeminarVerlag Basel, www.das-seminar.ch, also available in Kindle or other E-reader formats.

40. Werner Schäfer in *Gegenwart* no. 1/2011.

41. For more information on the work of Jan Stuten, I refer here to the detailed account in Wolfgang Veit, *Bewegte Bilder — der Zyklus 'Metamorphosen der Furcht' von Jan Stuten. Entwurf zu einer neuen Licht-Spiel-Kunst nach einer Idee von Rudolf Steiner*, Verlag Urachhaus, 1993.

42. See note 48 and the essay by Hans Jenny (physician, painter and founder of 'Cymatics'), 'Eine Methode, bewegliche Farbformen im Bühnenraum zu erzeugen', in *Bühnentechnische Rundschau*, 62nd year, issue 6, Berlin 1968.

43. See the reproduction of four of the sketches in the colour plates.

44. In 1999, *Fantasia 2000* appeared, as a result of many years' dogged work by Disney's nephew Roy Disney.

45. A. Tarkovsky, *Die versiegelte Zeit — Gedanken zur Kunst, zur Ästhetik und Poetik des Films*, Ullstein 1984, p. 126 ff and p. 192ff.

46. The unsettling aspect of this is something that Plato addressed already in his metaphor of the cave. Those imprisoned in the cave by their own thoughts bring to bear on the figures of their illusory world feelings that would be justified only in relation to the archetypes. They do not succeed in meeting the reflected images in an appropriate way. Or, as Balázs said: 'The suggestion of the film depends upon erasing the illusory character of its presentation'.

47. See p. 30.

48. The objective of the Berlin Association for Promoting Film founded by Wolfgang Otto Pfeiffer.

49. In a lecture given in Dornach (Switzerland) on 13 May 1921.

50. The police force in certain Swiss cantons use a software named Precobs whose statistical parameters enable them to enforce security measures in communities and areas previously much affected by

theft. In its issue of 29.11.2017, the daily newspaper *Blick* reported on this 'clairvoyant software'.

51. Such as Tarkovsky's *Solaris* (1972) or *The Eternal Sunshine of the Spotless Mind* (2004) by Michel Gondry (with Jim Carey and Reese Witherspoon).

52. As propounded by Hans Moravec, John Smart, Raymond Kurzweil (for some years now director of Goole's research department), Elon Musk and his neuralink project etc.

53. In Hans Moravec, *Computer übernehmen die Macht, vom Siegeszug der künstlichen Intelligenz*, Hamburg 1999.

54. More on this can be found at: http://www.zeitpunkt.ch/news/artikel-einzelansicht/artikel/krieg-der-goetter.html

55. *Berliner Zeitung*, 12 November 2009.

56. Tarkovsky, *Die versiegelte Zeit*, Ullstein 1984, p. 203. (*Sculpting in Time*, University of Texas Press 1989).

57. On the Savoldelli DVD, SeminarVerlag, www.das-seminar.ch

58. Tarkovsky, op. cit., p. 30.

59. Tarkovsky, op. cit., p. 189.

60. See also Savoldelli, 'Zur mediumistischen Nature des Kinos', 1983, text no. 10 in the digitalshop at www.das-seminar.ch

61. Already in his *Goethe's Theory of Knowledge — An Outline of the Epistemology of His Worldview*, written in 1886, the 25-year-old Steiner undertook to describe the counterstream between shaping ideas, or expressively (conceptually) engendered contents, and impressively (observationally) discovered sense perceptions.

62. Tarkovsky, op. cit, p. 126.

63. Tarkovsky, op. cit., p. 113.

64. We can recall here B. Balázs's formulation about the 'redemption of outer reality from the chaos of the random and transient', see p. 13.

65. Their famous 'L'arrivé du train' (1897) also stands as a figure for the transience of all cinematically recordable physicality in *Stella da Falla*.

66. See notes 38 and 39.

67. Eco's novel, *The Name of the Rose*, relates the behind-the-scenes story of the battle fought in the Middle Ages between those who regarded human ideas (which were called universals) as being in relationship with a world of spiritual reality (called Realists), and the others, amongst whom the author counts himself, embodied in his protagonist William of Baskerville, to whom ideas and concepts

appear as linguistic signs with no correspondence to any content that points beyond them (called Nominalists). The title of the novel refers to the hexameter line by Bernard of Cluny, 'Stat Rosa prostina nomine, nomina nuda tenemus.' ('The rose of long ago stands only here as name; it is only bare names that remain with us in the end'.)

68. The 'general semiology' required by Pasolini as a 'language of reality' was referred to by Herbert Witzenmann as 'egomorphosis of language'. He described its metamorphic affinity with the idea of destiny and reincarnation in *Die Kategorienlehre Rudolf Steiners*, Gideon-Spicker Verlag, Dornach.

69. PP. Pasolini, 'Anmerkungen zur Einstellungssequenz', published in Reihe Hanser, *Film 12*, p. 77.

70. The film *The Final Cut* (2004) by Omar Naïm, with Robin Williams, takes place in a future when people possess implants that record their whole life through their eyes. Socially high status 'cutters' use this 'life footage' to create a final cut or concluding film, freed of anything morally dubious, for the mourners and celebrants. The code of honour of these cutters includes, among other things, possessing no implants themselves (since all the life memories of their clients could be reconstructed from them, in unexpurgated form) and storing and selling no memories. Thus a final cut, with the aid of ahrimanically distorted technology, presents a falsified counter-image of the process after death as Pasolini invokes it.

71. Rudolf Steiner's spiritual science describes this 'concluding montage' as a post-mortem panorama or life review that lasts for roughly 72 hours, and contains an ever expanding, gradually weakening and dissolving, retrospective memory tableau of the person who has died. In his accounts of karma, Steiner also describes exercises that enable a person to perceive the karmic background that triggers them even while they are occurring.

72. Quoted in Thomas Assheuer, 'Zum Tod von Eric Rohmer', in *Zeit-Online*, 12 January 2010.

73. I asked the festival office whether it could disclose the views and evaluations of specific jury members, but received an answer in the negative.

74. Andrei Tarkovsky, *Die versiegelte Zeit*, Ullstein 1984, p. 159. (*Sculpting in Time*, University of Texas Press 1989)

75. Ibid., p. 208.

76. Ibid., p. 76.

77. As a 16-year-old, already — as I was reminded by the Swiss film director Clemens Klopfenstein in the festschrift for the 20th Solothurn film festival, *The show must go on … 1966–1985* (p. 37) — heavily symbolic film-shots and sequences were anathema to me. I had forgotten the incident that Klopfenstein records as follows:
'During the first Swiss film weeks, which took place in run-down health resorts, and were run by film-enthusiast teachers, things were pretty adolescent and ragged. I recall with mischievous pleasure how guest speaker Freddy Buache [founder and for many years director of Cinémathèque Suisse in Lausanne — author's note], interrupted the screening of Thérèse Desqueroux, and got the furious Savoldelli ejected from the hall because, each time a rainy window, a locked door or an expiring candle was shown, he had shouted out loudly, "Symbol, symbol"!'

78. Op. cit., p. 226.

79. Ibid., p. 65.

80. See the two photos in the colour plate section.

81. Op. cit., p. 70.

82. Ibid., p. 113.

83. See R.A. Savoldelli, 'Poesie — die Sprache des magischen Idealismus (die Wiederverienigung von Kunst und Wissenschaft bei Novalis)', text 119 in the digitalworkshop at www.das-seminar.ch

84. In the chapter 'The Metamorphosis of World Phenomena', In Rudolf Steiner *Goethe's Worldview*, first published in Weimar in 1897, GA 6.

85. Op. cit., p. 43.

86. Ibid., p. 69.

87. Ibid., p. 88.

88. Ibid., p. 188.

89. See page 71.

90. Op. cit. 184/185.

91. Ibid., p. 195.

92. Ibid., p. 49.

93. Interview with Gawan Fagard. See 'Die Fliege im Bernstein' on Kluge's website www.kluge-alexander.de

94. One-take films make do with single takes. Their remarkable fascination, arising from the virtual unity of space/time, has in recent years led to new experiments in the genre, first established

by Alfred Hitchcock with *Rope* ('A Cocktail for a Corpse') in 1948. In planned film-length sequences, the film director's visual artistry is required less than his choreographic and organizational talents. Instances from recent years are: Alexander Sokurov's *Russian Ark*, 2002, which was shot using around 1500 actors in 45 rooms of the St. Petersburg Hermitage, and for the first time undertook feature film recording directly on eight HDTV disks. Only four hours were available for the shoot, thus allowing only one pass; the Iranian film *Fish and Cat* (2013) by Shahram Mokri, and the Berlin film *Victoria* (2016) by Sebastian Schipper, are further examples of this singular type of cinematic entertainment.

95. Exceptions to this can be found in experimental films in which the cinematic idea is not based on a narrative that takes account of the continuity of space/time. One such, a film highly regarded at the time, was my film *LYDIA* (1968) (see www.HieronymusFilm.ch).

96. R. Steiner, lecture 6 of the Tone Eurythmy Course, 25 February 1924.

97. A detailed account of the transformation of musical intervals into eurythmy can be found in 'Ein toneurythmisches Kapitel' in Savoldelli, *Bedingungen eurythmischer Kultur — bewegtes Denken und beseelte Bewegung*, Verlag Freies Geistesleben, Stuttgart 1989.

98. www.Filmgeist.org

99. W.O. Pfeiffer, *Bigger Than Life*, Filmgeist-Verlag, Berlin 2017, p. 9.

100. Op. cit., p. 128.

101. Ibid., p. 125.

102. Ibid., p. 122.

103. Ibid., p. 130. See 'General Thoughts on Film' (in the appendix) and the agreement there expressed with this quotation.

104. Cf. what was said in this regard about Éric Rohmer.

105. Op. cit., p. 129.

106. See note 103.

107. Previously Kluge had assigned what he calls epiphany not to images but to their interrelationship through montage.

108. If the artist neglects to raise into consciousness what in former eras remained subconscious artistic creativity, but instead tries to kindle this approach anew, from his 'gut' — which may sometimes require his partial loss of control under the influence of a drug (alcohol, cannabis etc.), he is contributing in his particular field to symptoms of decline in modern art.

109. Op. cit., p. 125.

110. The modern aesthetics of Herbert Witzenmann in his *Die Philosophie der Freiheit als Grundlage künslterischen Schaffens*, Gideon Spicker Verlag 1984, still remains unsurpassed in showing how artistic perception can provide the germ of a universal aesthetics that extends and develops Schiller's basic ideas.

111. See the Wikipedia entry on 'Benjamin Libet'.

112. Such findings, accumulating more or less 'automatically' due to the huge financial resources directed toward this research, were 'filed away' almost unremarked following the (still ongoing) 'triumphant march' of gene technology (promoted with similarly exorbitant outlay and highly dubious results). The governments of the western world made these funds available for brain research between 1990 and 1999, after the US President George H.W. Bush — a suspect figure in many respects — launched the 'decade of the brain' in the summer of 1990 with his Executive Order no. 6158.

113. See Rudolf Steiner, *The Philosophy of Freedom*, Part I.

114. In appendix 3, on 'The Abstract Nature of Concepts' in his book *Riddles of the Soul* (1917), Rudolf Steiner describes in detail the process whereby our relationship to a purely spiritual thought essence of the world, with which we are unconsciously bound up in sense life, is dulled or dimmed into the recallable thoughts of body-supported consciousness.

115. At the beginning of the chapter 'The Idea of Freedom'.

116. More details on this in 'Some Effects of Initiation' In Rudolf Steiner, *Knowledge of the Higher Worlds* (1904).

117. This started already with the father of ecclesiastical Latin, Tertullian, around 200 AD: 'The Son of God is dead; this is fully believable because it is idiocy. And having been buried he rose again; this is certain, because it is impossible.'

118. Cf. 'In future I will write nothing but poetry — the sciences must all be poeticized; and I hope to speak with them a great deal of this real, scientific poetry...' And in a letter to A.W. Schlegel on 24.2.1798: 'The human world is the communal organ of the gods. Poetry unites them, as it does us.'

119. R. Steiner, Leading Thought Letter, 'Human Freedom and the Michael Age'.

120. See also the appendix of this book.

121. See p. 22.
122. Examples of this can be found in actors of Hong Sang-Soo's films, for instance Kim Min-Hee.
123. Surveys conducted over the last few years in Germany have found that the majority of people agree with this statement.
124. A little animal rights anecdote here: box-office takings for the film were reduced in the US by the fact that an animal protection organization refused to give the film a clean bill of health. A leaked video showed that the dog's second incarnation, a German Shepherd in the role of a police dog in Chicago, had to suffer a very unpleasant situation in a wild river torrent. Seemingly the production team were unable to get a stunt-dog quickly enough.
125. Thus the creation of cross-fade-free analogue projection, as the Skladanowsky brothers attempted it in their Duplex process (see page 7), did not involve great technical problems. Forty years ago this was confirmed to me, with the aid of a technical sketch, by the then director of the research and development department of the Swiss manufacturer of the much-loved BOLEX camera. In the end-phase of analogue technology, entrepreneurial interest — i.e. money — was lacking for such developments.
126. The Digital Cinema Initiatives (DCI) concluded in March 2002 by all the major Hollywood studios (Disney, Fox, MGM, Paramount, Sony Pictures, Universal and Warner Bros) created the basis for the global digitalization of production and film distribution that swiftly followed.
127. P.P. Pasolini, conversation with R. Schär, 1970, in *Cinema*, Zurich July 1976.
128. Ibid., p. 129.
129. Goethe has Mephisto say, in Auerbach's cellar: 'The people never feel the devil's touch, not even if he grasps them by the collar.'
130. Herbert Witzenmann, *Vererbung und Wiederverkörperung des Geistes*, Gideon-Spicker Verlag, p. 85.
131. In Orthology Seminars, run in Switzerland and Berlin, I spoke of this fundamental rhythm as the contemporary *new yoga,* one that replaces the now long-vanished possibility (due to changes in our corporeality over centuries and millennia) of attaining spiritual knowledge through control of the breathing.
132. See the Huston quotation on p. 11.

133. See the quotation on p. 22.

134. Herbert Witzenmann, op. cit., in the chapter 'Vom Ursprung der menschlichen Fähigkeiten'.

135. Otto Foulon, *Die Kunst des Lichtspiels*, 1924: from the eulogy given before the cremation of the light artist Matthias Grüner on 22 May.

136. In R.A. Savoldelli, 'Nur das Persönliche ist das Allgemeine', in the festschrift *The show must go on*, celebrating 20 years of the Solothurn Film Days in 1985 (edited by Ivo Kummer and Heinz Urben).

137. Rudolf Steiner established a modern, observation-based (post-Kantian) epistemology in his fundamental works *Goethe's Worldview*, *Truth and Science* and *The Philosophy of Freedom*. Herbert Witzenmann carried this work forward in the volumes *Strukturphänomenologie*, *Die Voraussetzungslosigkeit der Anthroposophie*, *Goethes universalästhetischer Impuls* and *Sinn und Sein*.

138. This motto from Goethe's *Faust*, which has become a mantra for many new-age meditators, is sometimes regarded as Faust's wisdom or even wrongly attributed to Goethe himself. In fact, it is part of a conversation with Mephistopheles in which Faust rejects this temptation: 'Should I speak to the moment, say: "Oh tarry do, so lovely as you are", then you might bind and chain me; and if so, then, I'll willingly be destroyed!'

139. Technical media means here the broadcasting of recorded auditory and visual sense perceptions to as many recipients as desired.

140. This remark appeared on 12 April 1925 in the weekly periodical *Das Goetheanum*, in Dornach, Switzerland.

141. Consciousness of movements is not based entirely on the sense of vision, however. Even a fly buzzing past the back of my head is perceived, not only through the acoustic modulations it causes but also by these being transferred with high precision into a spatialized movement (a fact that Dolby Surround and Skywalker Sound apply to their digital spatial recreation).

142. The beginning of Chapter 4: 'The World as Sense Perception'.

143. In the chapter 'The World as Sense Perception'.

144. This is why inner judgements of the 'I' are associated with forms of satisfaction or dissatisfaction. One says, perhaps, 'I am not pleased with myself', and this points to the field of tension between the I's true being and our usual picture of the I.

145. I only became acquainted with the works of Rudolf Steiner several years after this was written, and at the time had no knowledge of a comment such as the following, which bears a resemblance to what I was attempting here: 'On earth the I was a point, as it were. Here, between death and rebirth it is reflected everywhere from the peripheral circumference... and then one has one's previous lives really as in a mighty, outspread mirroring instrument...' (Rudolf Steiner in *Karmic Relationships*, Volume 1, GA 236).

A note from the publisher

For more than a quarter of a century, **Temple Lodge Publishing** has made available new thought, ideas and research in the field of spiritual science.

Anthroposophy, as founded by Rudolf Steiner (1861-1925), is commonly known today through its practical applications, principally in education (Steiner-Waldorf schools) and agriculture (biodynamic food and wine). But behind this outer activity stands the core discipline of spiritual science, which continues to be developed and updated. True science can never be static and anthroposophy is living knowledge.

Our list features some of the best contemporary spiritual-scientific work available today, as well as introductory titles. So, visit us online at **www.templelodge.com** and join our emailing list for news on new titles.

If you feel like supporting our work, you can do so by buying our books or making a direct donation (we are a non-profit/ charitable organisation).

office@templelodge.com

TEMPLE LODGE
For the finest books of Science and Spirit